MW00422737

Enterprise Content Strategy

A Project Guide

Kevin P. Nichols

Foreword by Ann Rockley

The Content Wrangler
Content Strategy Series

Enterprise Content Strategy
A Project Guide
Copyright © 2015 Kevin P. Nichols

Credits

Series Producer and Editor:	Scott Abel
Series Editor:	Laura Creekmore
Series Cover Designer:	Marc Posch
Indexer:	Cheryl Landes
Copy Editor:	Marcia Riefer Johnston
Illustrations:	Karen Machart
Publisher:	Richard Hamilton

Disclaimer

Trademarks

XML Press
Laguna Hills, California
http://xmlpress.net

First Edition
978-1-937434-44-1 (print)
978-1-937434-45-8 (ebook)

Table of Contents

Foreword

Just a few short years ago, content strategy was new and nebulous. People had heard the term, liked the idea, but there wasn't a lot of in-depth information on what it was, why do it, how to convince management, and how to get guidance on what to do. And although content strategy is now an accepted best practice and people understand what it is and why they need to do it, the how remains a challenge.

Enterprise Content Strategy: A Project Guide does an excellent job of answering the how.

Kevin draws on his years of practical experience developing content strategies, and in particular, he draws on his experience building, managing, and guiding one of the world's largest content strategy teams. He lives and breathes content strategy with some of the largest brands in the world. His experience educating and preparing his team on how to create an effective content strategy shines through in this book.

He has distilled his knowledge into a practical, hands-on book that is jam-packed full of definitions, questions you need to ask, checklists, and guidelines. He focuses not on the what or why, but on the how.

That's not to say that *Enterprise Content Strategy: A Project Guide* doesn't provide concepts. Kevin includes definitions at the beginning of each chapter to ensure that your understanding of the terminology is in alignment with the book, and he clearly explains some of the thornier concepts, such as responsive vs. adaptive design and multichannel vs. omnichannel. He adds examples that make the distinctions crystal clear.

Content strategy is typically focused on a single area, such as marketing, and on one or two channels, such as desktop web and mobile, but content strategy can extend further into a company's reach. It can extend into social media (Twitter, Facebook, Pinterest, etc.), into print (catalog, brochure), and frequently into video and podcasts. It can also extend into other channels, such as broadcast and radio. Enterprise content strategy addresses content strategy through the customer continuum, ranging from pre-sales to sales to product support, and it extends across many audiences, both internal and external. This book helps you to understand that big picture and the needs of the whole while focusing on the specifics of good content strategy.

But have no fear, even if you aren't responsible for an enterprise content strategy, but rather on a more focused content strategy, this book is also for you. The best practices and steps involved in enterprise content strategy are the same for any content strategy, just on a larger scale.

This book will become one of your most influential resources, bookmarked and highlighted on every page!

Ann Rockley
President,
The Rockley Group, Inc.

Preface

Content – websites, films, images, books, videos, articles ... content of any kind – can improve people's lives. Content can transform a brand or an organization. For starters, of course, the content has to be good by the appropriate standards. You can find resources galore on how to create good content. This book is not one of those resources.

What about the behind-the-scenes mechanisms and insights required to deliver a company's content at the right times and in the right ways? What about the complex, robust processes required to define, design, implement, and support that content? What about all the conversations and decisions that go into giving customers and potential customers business-enhancing ways to engage with all that content?

In short, what about enterprise content strategy?

That's where this book comes in.

Content strategy may not seem as sexy or intriguing as the content itself. I have heard some professionals in the digital industry – copywriters, creative directors, interaction designers – call content strategy boring. I've heard marketing directors say, "We don't need content strategy. We just need good content." It took me years to understand why they felt this way: their concern lay with content in its final form. I finally realized that when I work with these professionals, I need to connect the dots between content as a deliverable (in its final state) and the strategy behind that deliverable.

I wrote the first version of this book in 2007 as a checklist of best practices for anyone interested in content strategy. My friend Alexa O'Brien spent hours helping me fashion that list into something useful. I intended to publish the list on my website, but I never did. In 2010 at Sapient, I updated the list with the help of two peers, Julie Christie and Laura Lerner, who reworked the entire narrative. Again, work and excuses got the best of me, and nothing was published. Later, another friend, Rebecca Schneider, reviewed many iterations and provided feedback. Last year, when Scott Abel invited me to write a book, I sent him the manuscript. He and Ann Rockley encouraged me to develop it into a book. Laura Creekmore then suggested that I restructure the best practices into a project guide.

You are now reading the culmination of all those efforts.

This book is prescriptive. I drive right into the how-to with little pre-amble. I set out to create something succinct and practical, a peek into what I've learned during my many years of doing this kind of work.

The term *enterprise* in my title may seem to imply that I'm addressing only companies above a certain size. Not so. This book is for anyone who wants to understand and reap the business benefits of content strategy.

This book follows in a tradition created by other authors, most notably Ann Rockley, whose definitive guide, *Managing Enterprise Content: A Unified Content Strategy*[17], is a must-read for anyone who wants to understand this topic. Ann's work has inspired me throughout my career. Many principles outlined here owe their existence to her longstanding contributions to this field. Countless other authors and practitioners have also taught me along the way. In writing this book, I add my voice to the voices of many who have shared what they know about the strategic side of this exciting business. May you find something here that enables you and your teams to produce effective, relevant, timely content that helps your enterprise – whatever it may be – flourish.

CHAPTER 1
Definitions and Approach to Enterprise Content Strategy

Within the digital and interactive world, content strategists continue to discuss how to define content strategy. Even the term *content* has many definitions. In this chapter, you will learn how to define content, what enterprise content strategy is, a recommended approach for building an enterprise content strategy framework, and when to engage an enterprise content strategist. I also discuss several ways to approach a project.

This chapter also covers the role of omnichannel and omnichannel implications for content strategy, particularly enterprise content strategy.

What does content mean?

In 2013, Rebecca Schneider[1] and I came up with this definition:

> **Content:** any information that someone records.

Period. Within this definition, many things qualify as content:

- A YouTube video featuring mountain goats scaling a vertical mountain cliff (yes, those goats can do that)
- One of the few existing audio recordings of Virginia Woolf discussing the concept of words
- Hieroglyphics from ancient Egypt showcasing Queen Nefertiti
- Cave paintings of reindeer from the Neolithic era in Lascaux (which scholars recently concluded to be the works of women, not men, calling into question that whole hunters-as-male thing)
- Omar Khayyam's *Rubáiyát* written in the 11th century
- Édouard-Léon Scott de Martinville's first recorded sound (nearly ten seconds of a woman singing "Au Clair de la Lune")
- Fritz Lang's film, *Metropolis*
- A book review in the *New York Times*
- Any type of interactive experience, such as the United Nations website
- The latest reality TV show, such as *Dance Moms*

---

[1] http://azzardconsulting.com

Content today includes text, images, video, audio, and digital assets such as PDFs, multimedia, rich media, social media, and metadata.

Regardless of its varied manifestations, content has certain characteristics:

- Content captures an instance of information read, seen, or heard at least once.
- Content has a creator and a consumer. (The creator may be the only consumer.)
- A consumer's perceptions create and derive meaning and relevance from content, which may or may not adhere to the creator's intent.

Content communicates information and manifests an experience or relationship with a content consumer. The best way to define digital content is as follows:

> Information created by someone and stored in a digital format with the capability of being shared (or not) in the future.

This book focuses primarily on content in the context of a brand's or organization's identity. Because of this focus, any content produced by an enterprise is, by definition, a business or organizational asset.

Created properly, content can have a definitive value associated with it, such as the monetary or brand value it brings to an organization. Good content can lead to better recognition of a brand, contribute to an organization's mission, raise funds, or generate revenue. Next to products and services, content exists as the face of a brand or organization. Any brand or organization can harness significant power from good content.

Content and the content experience

When consumed, content creates an experience for the consumer. The term *consumer* in this context includes anyone who consumes content, whether internal or external to an organization, through any platform.

This book uses the term consumer instead of end user since end user can imply interaction on levels beyond passive consumption of content. For example, a consumer could be someone who reads text from a user guide but does not necessarily interact with a digital experience. A consumer can also be anyone who calls a product-support center. In this scenario, a specialist, guided by content served up on a company's internal portal, serves a customer's needs or requests.

The term *experience* may seem powerful as well as ambiguous. *Experience* conveys the emotional response a consumer has when engaging with content and the mental experience it creates. To explain this concept a bit further, consider the following:

- How do you feel and what experience does a beautiful song create the first time you hear it?
- How do you feel and what experience do you have when you read a compelling novel?
- What emotional response surfaces and how do you perceive your experience with a brand and its product when the company's website lacks the information you need?
- How satisfied does a call to a customer support center feel when you get everything you need in a timely manner, leaving you able to resolve an issue?
- When you view a television commercial for a nonprofit organization, then to go a website and see all the amazing work the organization does to better humanity, how inspired are you?

The content experience includes every piece of content with which a consumer interacts that reflects the organization or brand – regardless of whether that content was created by the organization or by other parties and consumers. For example, the content experience can include what others say about the brand or organization through social channels like Twitter or what influencers write about a product in a blog.

In the relationship between a brand or organization and the consumer, the content experience constitutes the consumer's interaction with usable, timely, and branded content at every distribution-exchange point where consumers access information. In this context, when we think of content as active engagement – as opposed to a passively consumed, static piece of information – the increased value of content to an organization and to the person who consumes it becomes clear.

Because of the experience that content creates – bad or good – content creates a life-force for a brand. Content can mean success, or failure.

What is enterprise content strategy?

What if you wrote and recorded a potentially multiplatinum, Grammy-winning song, but it never made it to iTunes, the airways, or store shelves, so no one ever heard it? Without an effective way to deliver your masterpiece and get it heard, you may be the only person to ever appreciate it. Without a publishing platform to offer it and market it to those who have not heard it, your exposure will be limited.

Put another way, a brand may have the best product, but without the proper messaging, the content to support the product, and the ability to reach consumers, the company that developed the product may end up bankrupt. A competitor may rise up and succeed solely because it has better content. Content can make or break a brand, and it can determine whether an NGO or nonprofit succeeds.

A content strategy proves critical. Good content in and of itself can no longer be the only goal. Businesses must have a content strategy to identify new content opportunities, create new content, optimize existing content, and deliver content to the right audience. Within this dynamic, the content itself and how well it can be delivered, found, seen, experienced, and improved upon are the keys to success for any organization.

Steven Grindlay, a content strategist in Montreal, says,

> Where there is communication, there is content. There is ample evidence in the pre-Internet past that companies used content in marketing, advertising, and PR to establish a competitive advantage. In particular, this was the case with products perceived to be commodities, for example: petroleum products, alcoholic beverages, and tires.
>
> Every organization engages in a wide variety of internal and external communications with consumers and stakeholders. Taken as a whole this communication exerts enormous influence on behalf of the enterprise and its brands.
>
> —Steven Grindlay, private communication

In 2006, I stated in articles and conference presentations that "content strategy is best defined with the precept of 'how to get the right content, to the right user, at the right time.'" Since then, this phrase has been co-opted and borrowed by others in the digital and interactive industry. "Right content, right user, right time" gets thrown around a lot nowadays to describe anything from content strategy and good visual design to content marketing strategy.

Given that so many other disciplines have appropriated my notion, last year I decided it was time to refactor the definition. In 2013, Anne Casson (Director of Content Strategy at SapientNitro) and I published a refined definition of content strategy:

> Content Strategy is the systematic, thoughtful approach to surfacing the most relevant, effective, and appropriate content at the most opportune time, to the appropriate user, for the purpose of achieving a company's strategic business objectives and its customers' goals. It is an overarching strategy that is realized fully only through many deliverables and tactics that touch many different people, processes, systems, and customer targets.
>
> —*SapientNitro Content Strategy 2013 Positioning*[5]

Enterprise content strategy envelops all proprietary and intellectual property across an organization's operational infrastructure. It includes every method used to deliver content to the consumer and all the interaction and integration points.

Enterprise content strategy considers all delivery platforms or exchange experiences (digital, web, mobile, telephony, catalog, print, broadcast, kiosk, or virtual exchange point); all content formats and types (text, video, audio, or brand experience); and all content consumers and audiences (customer, employee, career-seeker, vendor, or investor). An enterprise content strategy includes and influences them all.

The activities of an enterprise content strategy do not live within one project. Instead, many separate projects can potentially contribute to a strategy's success. For example, the roll-out of an e-commerce website might include a content management system (CMS), an analytics tool to measure its performance, a personalization engine, a campaign-management application, and various other tools. The e-commerce website might link to a product database and pull content from a variety of sources. (Later chapters detail each of these concepts.)

Fundamentally, enterprise content strategy comprises three factors:

- **Content experience:** How does the organization define the content experience and determine which stories need to be told, including every type of content that people see, hear, or interact with?
- **Content delivery:** Which processes acquire, create, review, publish, evaluate, optimize, maintain, and (eventually) archive content?
- **Content governance:** What operational and organizational processes sustain the success of content (and are necessary to do so)?

Each aspect presents complexities. All three break down into a series of business processes and tools to properly execute them.

I want to point out an issue some of you may be seeing: What if you are focused on one project and consider it to be channel-specific content strategy work (such as the development of a new desktop website) as opposed to *enterprise* content strategy work? Since content strategy best practices and approaches are the same as those found within enterprise content strategy (with enterprise accounting for more variables), any content strategy or strategist will benefit from the principles outlined in this book.

One more point of clarification. Today we have websites, mobile smartphone and tablet sites, and various types of digital interactions in stores, taxicabs, and airports (to name just a few). Content publishing becomes more complicated as new technologies emerge. But the basic principles have existed for years. The way a newspaper, magazine, television network, or company created information around a product fifty years ago still proves relevant today. Then, as now, content was all about creating a meaningful and relevant experience for the consumer. These organizations had robust processes to deliver content and a means to govern quality and distribution.

We may face different technologies today, but these principles still apply.

Understanding the enterprise content strategy project lifecycle

When we begin a technology-related project, we create a series of phases within a project plan to execute the work. Sometimes these phases are known as plan, discover, define, design, implement, deploy, and support.

Since enterprise content strategy also encompasses specific processes, I have created a lifecycle process specific to content that includes seven basic phases of work: plan, assess, define, design, build, publish, measure, and optimize. Figure 1.1 shows these phases as a closed loop with governance at the center.

The next section, "Phases and objectives of an enterprise content strategy," describes the phases of the content strategy project lifecycle. Later chapters explore each phase in detail.

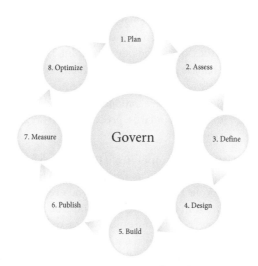

Figure 1.1 – Content strategy project lifecycle

Phases and objectives of an enterprise content strategy

Phase	Objective
Plan	Define what will happen in the project at a high level, and create parameters around the team structure and budget.
Assess	Identify and survey the content ecosystem:

Identify and survey the content ecosystem:

- **Business goals and objectives:** How effectively does the content help your business or organization meet its goals and objectives?
- **Effectiveness, relevance, quality, and timeliness of the content itself:** Define the ideal experience for a content consumer with the types of content to support it.
- **User feedback:** What are users saying about the content through surveys, customer call centers, or social channels like Facebook or Twitter?
- **Analytics inputs:** What can you glean from web analytics, content testing, or any other sources of data on content performance?
- **Competitive analysis:** What types of content do your competitors provide or not provide? How can you do it better?

- **Survey of technology:** Can the current technology support your goals and objectives? Are there any gaps, issues, or technology constraints?
- **Analysis or audits of internal processes:** How effectively are you delivering content?
- **Governance evaluation:** Are you governing content through standards, processes, and organizational structures?

Define   Gather all the inputs from the assess phase to determine what you need to do for the future. This phase frames the project by defining what you need to do with content. From this phase, you should be able to identify high-level goals and objectives for one or more projects. You should provide enough detail to procure budgets for the project as well as inform any requirements that the project teams will need to consider, including which technology needs to be used and the project scope.

If you understand project management principles, you will be able to produce a definitive scope, business requirements, and a mid-level project plan from this phase in preparation for design activities.

Design   Design the future-state experience. Depending on which projects and work are identified, this phase includes many activities. Think of this phase as designing the necessary future-state experience, such as what content and information go on a website or what content is required for a user guide that accompanies a new product.

Implement   Build and execute the design. Working with a technology team, develop and implement the projects. You may also migrate existing content into a new website or work with teams to finalize the content that needs to go into any final experience.

Publish   Distribute the content to a consumer. In many cases, this phase consists of a series of ongoing steps. For example, a magazine will publish some content monthly and some daily to a website. This phase also includes the maintenance of any existing content. You may also have to review and moderate user-generated content, such as comments, ratings, or reviews.

Measure   Evaluate the performance of your content. Assess what content people consume, share in social networks like Facebook, and comment on. Also identify which content meets your business goals and which does not.

Optimize   Review the findings from the measure phase to make recommendations. Decide which content to invest in. Address new business needs, and identify areas within the content experience to improve and optimize.

Govern   Develop a governance model to ensure that you have effective standards, processes, people, and organizational structures in place so you can maintain the effectiveness of all phases.

Putting these phases together creates a cyclical process. For example, once you launch a project, such as a new website, to consumers, you can use what you learn from measurements to improve the experience. We call this type of lifecycle a closed-loop process. In a closed-loop process, an experience never exists in a complete state; measurements and continual evaluation inform future priorities. You may have heard of performance-driven content, meaning content that an organization identifies and improves depending on how well that content performs. This closed-loop process provides the fuel behind performance-driven content.

A closed-loop lifecycle helps future-proof a project, keeping the outputs (in this case, content) relevant throughout the future. A successful and effective enterprise content strategy depends on continual evolution, and this approach makes that possible. A closed-loop process also ensures what we call *performance-driven content,* meaning content set up for evaluation and measurement so that an organization can improve it if necessary. Since we live in a world where new technology continues to emerge and existing technologies evolve, this type of process makes an organization more nimble in responding to future technology needs.

When to engage an enterprise content strategist

Often, the people engaged in projects that include content (any new product, website, or interactive experience) do not understand how, why, whether, or when to engage an enterprise content strategist, let alone the considerations for an enterprise content strategy. They may omit or poorly define major portions of content work within the project.

I have seen instances through the years where a creative team led the charge for a content experience and failed to bring in content experts until too late. In some cases, content seemed to magically appear as an afterthought, forcing the project to incur significant additional costs as a result.

If you are reading this book trying to determine whether you need an enterprise content strategist, here are some guidelines on the kinds of projects that should use one:

- Development of websites or multichannel solutions (mobile, in-store kiosks, etc.) that reach customers external to an organization
- Design or development of any aspect of a content lifecycle including migration, creation, acquisition, production, or publishing
- System-integration efforts with a focus on data exchange where information flows from one system to another (for example, customer relationship management (CRM) databases integrated with a customer call center and a external website)
- Projects with a *content management system* (CMS), digital asset management (DAM), search component, taxonomy, metadata, or dynamic navigation such as parametric navigation (filtered search)

Failing to account for the enterprise content strategy role poses significant risks to any future solutions. In 2013, Anne Casson and I wrote a paper on content strategy and SapientNitro.[2] Anne came up with this astonishing top-ten list of the things clients say that show they need a content strategist:

1. We don't know how much content we have.
2. We don't know every place our content is stored.
3. Our content is "all over the place."
4. We have homegrown content or systems to publish content.
5. We have not assigned owners to our content.
6. We know that our users see a link to a fee schedule from 1997 in search engine results.
7. We never delete anything, we just unlink it.
8. We have multiple copies of various things in our CMS.
9. It takes two weeks to make an editorial change to our website.
10. We know personalization is important, but we aren't sure where to start.

If you have heard people in your organization say any of these things, and you don't employ an enterprise content strategist, you should hire one and fast.

---

[2] *SapientNitro Content Strategy 2013 Positioning.* [5].

Future-proofing your solutions (aka performance-driven content)

Future-proofing represents another important concept within enterprise content strategy. Future-proofing content solutions means that you set up your content ecosystem to respond and adapt to change, namely, new technology, changing user behaviors, and organizational or business changes. A future-proofed solution creates a framework within an organization that minimizes rework of technology, business processes, and the content itself when advances change business needs.

This framework has two parts. The first part includes the processes and strategy necessary to support the framework. The closed-loop approach creates a sustainable framework to ensure success. Equally important, the second part includes how an organization organizes, structures, labels, and tags content.

Chapter 5, explores this area and some other key considerations. For the best resource on how to create a solid model, read Ann Rockley's *Managing Enterprise Content: A Unified Content Strategy*[17], which presents a thorough and meticulous approach.

Omnichannel and why it is critical

Omnichannel is not a synonym for *multichannel*. Multichannel means that more than one channel requires consideration or more than one channel exists within a content ecosystem. Generally speaking, a channel indicates a platform to deliver content. There are many types of channels. These are the primary external channels:

- Desktop (generally a website but includes any desktop file containing content)
- Mobile tablet (a website or app)
- Mobile smartphone of feature phone (a website or app)
- In-store (any in-store content materials, including content found on an end-cap, sales materials, or in-store kiosks)
- Publications (various but generally print publications not covered in any of these other categories)
- TV and radio (ads or programs)
- Product packaging (includes the box or labels and any in-the-box content like user guides, quick-start guides, or user manuals)
- Customer support (content necessary for call centers or online real-time customer-support agents)
- Digital billboards and signage
- Print (ads, articles, and brochures)

If multichannel means more than one channel, let us extend the concept to multichannel strategy, which indicates that an organization has developed a strategic approach to optimize content in each channel. An effective multichannel experience may strive to provide a collective content experience across all channels, taking advantage of each channel's unique strengths as well as cross-referencing experiences for each of the channels.

This approach used to work. But now, consumers interact with content in an always-on world with clear expectations of what each channel should provide them, and they expect timely content at all distribution points (mobile smartphone, desktop website, etc). Given the role of social media and other forms of user-generated content, the stakes have never been higher or more difficult to achieve.

Enter omnichannel.

Omnichannel, an approach to multichannel, provides tailored content at every point in the customer journey. In contrast to multichannel, omnichannel embodies an all-encompassing model to a consumer's experience with an organization or brand.

Martha Stewart is the mother of omnichannel experience. Before the term existed, she named her company Omnimedia. Stewart starts with stories related to her cookbooks, magazines, products, and do-it-yourself content. She then optimizes aspects of these stories through a variety of media: books, magazines, television programs, websites, mobile apps, and in-store experiences. Her TV show references her cookbooks, her magazine references both, and she fully realizes her content in multimedia and digital media. In each case she creates unique, channel-specific content that draws from the strength of the channel.

Today, we live in an always-on world with many ways to consume content. Grasping the concept of omnichannel is critical to supporting consumers' needs and differentiating your organization from the competition. Omnichannel provides content at every consumer touchpoint or channel and considers time, manner, and place. Omnichannel includes analog, digital, in-store, and person-to-person interactions.

Figure 1.2 shows a typical omnichannel customer lifecycle. Within this framework, you can see that the consumer engages with an experience through several channels and several engagements.

Figure 1.2 – Omnichannel customer lifecycle

Recently, people have said to me that omnichannel seems to apply to only big-brand experiences. I disagree. I think that this framework provides a critical understanding of a consumer's engagement with any brand or organization in terms of how he or she interacts with and uses online and offline content.

To apply an omnichannel approach to content strategy means that you consider every touchpoint and optimize it for a consumer's needs. You align your organization's goals with those of the consumer, and then provide content to meet those goals in each channel.

We can no longer design or plan for a single-channel experience because, like it or not, people consume our content in a variety of channels. Figure 1.3 presents the complexities of the world we now live in from an omnichannel perspective.

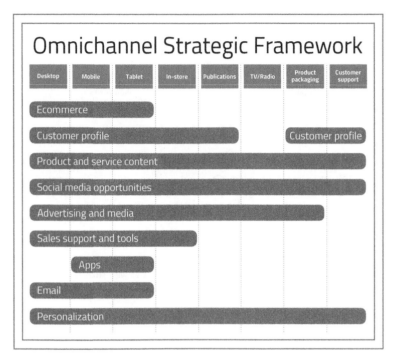

Figure 1.3 – Omnichannel framework

Chapter 5, *Design Phase*, shows how to use the omnichannel strategic framework to create a successful content solution.

Considerations for waterfall and agile projects

Although outside the scope of this guide, another clarification proves helpful in understanding enterprise content strategy. In technology project management, there are two primary types of project processes: waterfall and agile.

In the waterfall approach, a project has a series of phases: discover, define, design, implement, roll out, etc. Each phase contains discrete start and end dates, and each phase must be completed before the next begins.

Agile projects complete each phase rapidly, often in parallel with other phases, with several tracks of effort working simultaneously. For example, an effort to build an e-commerce shopping cart might run in parallel with an effort to build a website user profile.

For enterprise content strategy, both approaches can be effective. Whichever approach you use, I recommend completing a thorough assess phase prior to kicking off design activities.

In some cases, the current-state assessment, completed in the assess phase, can be specific to the deliverable itself. For example, a taxonomy-development effort could require a current-state analysis of the taxonomy and not the entire content ecosystem. However, consider this warning, which repeats throughout this book:

> The failure to complete a thorough assess phase will likely result in a failure to account for all the issues, gaps, and opportunities that the future-state design should address.

I have seen entire project delivery schedules delayed for months, resulting in multimillion-dollar cost overruns, because a quick-and-dirty content inventory missed significant amounts of hidden content – content that was necessary to migrate from the existing site to the new design.

The same holds true for those unfortunate content strategists who get thrown into a project – or, more likely, are identified as critical to the project – after that project somehow finds itself well underway. In this case – and given that many still consider content strategy nascent, this scenario will likely happen to you in your career – insist on a current-state assessment, even if it means explaining to your client or boss that you must do stakeholder interviews (after some may have been completed) or that this effort will affect a project's scope. Any deliverable outlined within the design phase must have a current-state assessment prior to initiating its development.

Additional reading

Ann Rockley and Charles Cooper's *Managing Enterprise Content: A Unified Content Strategy*[17] is arguably the best work on enterprise content management and strategy. Rockley wrote the first book on the topic and founded an entire practice around it.

A must-read for any content strategist practitioner on content strategy (and an overall primer on the subject) is *Content Strategy for the Web*[8] by Kristina Halvorson and Melissa Rach. Next to Ann Rockley, the practice of content strategy must recognize Halvorson and her determination, passion, and vision to bring the discipline to the forefront of business strategy and the digital industry. She has been a pioneer in this practice and continues to be so with her ConFab conferences and thought leadership. If Ann Rockley is the mother of content strategy, then Kristina Halvorson is a prophet who put content strategy on the map within the digital and interactive industry.

For a set of definitions and framework for content strategy contributed by industry experts, see *The Language of Content Strategy*[1] edited by Scott Abel and Rahel Bailie. This work provides a comprehensive set of terms and definitions on content strategy.

A strong work on business justification for content strategy, and perhaps the best book to position content strategy strategically in an organization, is *Content Strategy: Connecting the dots between business, brand, and benefits*[3] by Rahel Bailie and Noz Urbina.

A great read for any content strategist or aspiring practitioner is Margot Bloomstein's *Content Strategy at Work*[4]. She makes a case for where and how content strategy fits into interactive projects and provides examples of how to do it.

For a whitepaper on content strategy that succinctly defines when and how to use it and why it is important, see *SapientNitro Content Strategy 2013 Positioning*[5] by Anne Casson and Kevin Nichols.

Two great resources for content strategy overall:

Jonathon Colman's *Epic List of Content Strategy Resources*[6].

Content Strategy Alliance (contentstrategyalliance.com), provides a valuable resource to practitioners with ongoing updates for content strategy as a practice.

CHAPTER 2
Plan Phase

Enterprise content strategy projects always begin with a plan phase. For a new project, the plan phase helps sell the content work to the leaders and other decision makers in an organization. Planning also informs the scope of the effort necessary to execute the work.

For a publication process that uses a closed-loop approach, where an organization continually evaluates content and where new content areas are explored semiannually or quarterly, this phase identifies new content focus areas, such as a new section of a desktop website or an investment in an area of high-performing content. This phase can help an organization identify and agree on high-level organizational and consumer goals that content should meet, such as increased sales, reduction or resolution of pain points, improved customer engagement, or entrance into new markets.

As a caveat, all work and assumptions made within the plan phase should be validated at the end of the assess and define phases, as these phases will validate the details of the effort. The plan phase also includes setting up an appropriate team, constructing an objective and purpose for the work, and assessing high-level requirements. During the plan phase, you – assuming you are either the enterprise content strategist or the person responsible for content strategy – will also account for enterprise content strategy, ensuring adequate representation within the overall plan and strategy.

This chapter teaches you how to get started, build an appropriate team, set up the structure necessary to execute future phases, solicit the proper inputs, and create the right level of documentation to set the stage and scope of work. Finally, this chapter explores how to use the plan phase in an ongoing closed-loop approach.

Creating a content team

The team's primary objective: Make certain that the enterprise content strategy and the future-state experience account for the business, end-user, technology constraints, and information needs. For smaller organizations, use the information that follows as a guideline to represent the various considerations of content. Note that in many instances, one stakeholder will wear many hats, such as a webmaster who owns creating content for, designing, coding, and publishing an entire website.

Start by identifying the stakeholders necessary to construct a content team for the project. This content team acts as a subteam within the overall project framework. In internal projects, treat this as an internal client team. Expect eight to ten people on this team. If the size grows larger than ten, see if one person can represent more than one line of business (for example, one person for all of sales instead of two people representing sales of product X and sales of product Y). This will help keep the team as efficient as possible.

All stakeholders with an interest in content (marketing, web, social, communications, etc.) should be on – or represented in – this team.

One team member may represent the interests of several stakeholders, such as SEO, analytics, and taxonomy. Table 2.1 shows the responsibilities of team members.

Table 2.1 – Content team responsibilities

Area	Representative's responsibilities
Analytics	Ensures that the effort considers the input of web analytics, content analytics, user feedback, content performance, and usability.
Content lifecycle	Represents all areas of the content lifecycle, including acquisition, creation, entry into a CMS or DAM, review, maintenance, publication, evaluation, and optimization.
Content creation	Accounts for the needs of content creators. This content could include images and multimedia, such as videos.
Content management and editing	Represents editors in chief, content moderators, and content curators.
Business-unit content ownership	Covers the various lines of business to represent their needs and the way content functions within each product line or sales channel.
Content providing	Represents providers of any type of content, including content from syndication and third-party vendors.
International/regional management	Ensures international and regional (region can be any type of geographical region relevant to the organization) requirements and needs are considered.
Legal	Acts on behalf of legal interests and accounts for any legal, compliance, or regulatory concerns in content.

Area	Representative's responsibilities
Marketing and brands	Safeguards the interests of the brand in decisions and represents the needs of the marketing team(s).
Omnichannel/ multichannel	Represents channel needs, such as mobile smartphone, tablet, in-store, desktop website, e-mail, print, etc.
Personalization	Provides guidance on personalization.
Product line or sales	Represents the needs of product line and sales teams.
Search-engine optimization (SEO)	Represents the interests of SEO within consumer-facing, digital solutions, or any type of experience where search constitutes a component (including internal site search engines).
Taxonomy/metadata	Reviews and validates any decision affecting taxonomy, especially enterprise taxonomies. May also represent SEO and metadata.
Translation/localization/ internationalization	Provides expertise on decisions for international or global efforts. Required for organizations that produce content in more than one country.

To encourage alignment with other tracks of work, this team should also have a business analyst (BA) and a technology architect present during key deliverable reviews and major project checkpoints, and the BA and architect should be informed of all decisions from this group.

When any type of digital, interactive experience is designed, a member of the user experience (UX) team and an information architect need to be present. You may not require a UX, BA, or technology person in every team meeting, but these groups should be a part of all key deliverable reviews and key decisions.

If you are designing a new CMS or other type of technology solution, the project's technical architect should attend team meetings and understand the implications of decisions made by the team. Equally important, the content team must understand the technology requirements and constraints to avoid designing something that cannot be implemented; a technical architect can mitigate this risk.

As an additional decision factor in selecting team members, each team member should allocate sufficient time to meet weekly and to complete ongoing assignments. Otherwise, he or she must have the authority to delegate the work and ensure completion of all deliverables. These assignments will likely include work beyond each team member's current position. Thus, each member must commit to completing deliverables within the timeframe required. Because these members should weigh in on the timeframes, each should understand the commitments against deliverable dates.

The enterprise content strategist should lead this content team. An important piece in this leadership role, the entire team should view the content strategist as a service-oriented expert without ties to politics or cultures within the organization. A project manager sits on the team to take notes, create a plan from the scope and requirements work, and manage that process through each phase of work.

The content team's role in the organization

The content team functions as the primary resource for the development of all deliverables critical for the enterprise content strategy engagement. Therefore, the content team should be convened as soon as you recognize the need for an enterprise content strategy engagement. This team's existence ensures buy-in within the organization. It allows each line of business to provide input into all decisions.

In addition, the team ensures that each business unit is appropriately represented in the decisions. A multidisciplinary team of content stakeholders also guarantees a stronger, more effective content solution. A governance team, or stakeholders with appropriate authority, should approve the content team's decisions.

Setting up effective decision making

Content is political. Ironically, while it's nearly impossible to get people to recognize the value of content at certain points in a project, they will appear out of the woodwork to recognize its value when it comes to ownership.

To cut through the political and cultural noise and drive maximum efficiency, the content team should be defined and ruled by consensus. This practice fosters effective change management by depoliticizing decisions and minimizing the perception that cultural differences are tied to hierarchy or preferential treatment.

To facilitate this process, do the following:

- Define clear escalation points at the start of the project. Sometimes a consensus-driven structure will reach an impasse. When that happens, you may require arbitration by a higher authority, which in most cases will be a C-level executive or senior leader. The governance committee can also act in this role.

- Establish a protocol whereby each member meets with his or her business group and reviews the team's work, decisions, and deliverables. This approach creates a comfort level within each line of business and minimizes rumors and conjectures. This is an especially important step for key deliverables.

- Ask each team member to regularly solicit feedback and validation for all deliverables from his or her line of business. Because many deliverables are developed over time, each instance or version of the deliverable should include a review cycle within each line of business. This effort establishes early buy-in and minimizes issues during the rollout of the changes.

By following these three recommendations, the content team manages change in a healthy way from the beginning of the project and sets a precedent for positive, transparent action.

Identifying requirements

After securing the team, gather all content-related requirements. Requirements should include existing or known necessities as well as wish lists. They do not need to be detailed, but they should include any considerations or business knowledge necessary for the success of the project. They can also include any of the following documentation:

- Analytics
- Authoring standards
- Authoring templates or copy decks
- Branding guides
- Business objectives or goals
- CMS design documents, such as content models
- CMS/DAM system documentation
- Competitive analysis
- Content calendars
- Content inventories and audits
- Content lifecycle diagrams
- Content matrices
- Content or copy style guides

- Content strategy point of view
- Creative briefs or content briefs
- Editorial calendars
- Market-rollout matrixes
- Marketing and business objectives
- Metrics used to measure content or operational efficiency of publishing or data management
- Publication plans
- Publication processes and rules
- Search engine optimization (SEO) strategy
- Taxonomy and metadata standards or schemas
- Technological standards or constraints
- User or audience segments and personas
- User feedback on existing content

You may find only some of these documents – or none. If you have a fair number, do not fear a detailed analysis at this point. Use the following goal: Gather any relevant information with the expectation that further analysis will occur shortly thereafter.

Defining the project charter

Once they gather the necessary input, the team should define the project's charter: its goals, objectives, scope, deliverables, etc. To complete this effort, draw from the project brief, analytics, creative brief, business objectives, user requirements, and any other known requirements. As you survey these, work with the content team to define a project charter for the overall content model, structure, scope, and production processes. Table 2.2 shows the components of a project charter.

Table 2.2 – Project charter definition

Focus area	Definition
Goal	A goal sets the context for what a project should accomplish. A goal is general as well as visionary. The goal's purpose includes building enthusiasm and support for the project. An example of a goal is: *Build the most widely consumed content experience in our industry.* No details exist on how the goal will be accomplished: the goal stands alone as an inspirational directive to give the organization a benchmark toward which to aspire. As a best practice, you should limit your project to one or two goals, one primary and one secondary. Each should be followed with specific objectives.

Focus area	Definition
Objectives	An objective represents a specific and measurable focus area that can be reasonably accomplished. Example: Our new website will acquire twenty percent more users within six months of launch. For a discussion of both goals and objectives and how to define each, see Chapter 7, *Publish and Measure Phases*.
Purpose and high-level scope	The purpose and scope answer the following questions: ■ What are we doing? ■ Why are we doing this work? ■ For whom are we doing it, and which teams should be involved? ■ Where does the content reside (for example, which channels, such as desktop website, mobile smartphone, in store, internal publications, etc.)? ■ How does a consumer complete the task, or which tasks are necessary to complete the effort? ■ When must the work be completed? Best practices for scope definition include creating a comprehensive and accurate definition of the services, tasks, and deliverables that make up the project. Services, tasks, and deliverables should have well-defined parameters and ownership. Prioritize items within the scope and assign ownership for each service, task, and deliverable. Validate the overall scope at the end of the assess and define phases, because each of these phases will give you more details to hone in on as you define the scope of the project.
Project phases and deliverables	This component ties deliverables to each project phase. At this point, the plan will be very high level. Your team can also work with a project manager to set timing around the phases. However, realistically, the timing for phases cannot be finalized until the content team completes a full definition of the work required for the project.
Ownership of deliverables	All deliverables should have a specific owner. For example, the taxonomy lead owns the taxonomy.
Best practices	Any best practices or industry standards adopted by the organization and to which the team should conform. For example, some organizations use Six Sigma for any business process or operational procedure. For many teams, there may be none.

Focus area	Definition
Design principles	What are the design principles guiding the effort? Although you will revisit these during the design phase, you should map out and agree upon high-level principles to facilitate difficult decisions. Choose five to seven. Examples: ■ The user always remains at the center. ■ The solution must be nimble and adaptive. ■ We have no first channel; all necessary channels are relevant and we will optimize content for each. ■ Sustainability (as in maintainability of the content) informs all our decisions. ■ All content must be consistent, relevant, and timely. ■ Contextually relevant content frames the core of our strategic approach.
Dependencies, risks, and assumptions	Each task should contain dependencies (what is required to start or finish the task), assumptions (what does the team assume about the task), and identified risks. Work with a business analyst and project manager to determine each of these. Call out assumptions, expectations, dependencies, risks, and issues for each scope area.
Budget	If the team understands the budget or budget constraints, document them. If not, document projected costs.

One essential element of the project charter is a mapping of deliverables to phases, At SapientNitro we have defined a process that ties each deliverable to a phase of work for a typical content strategy project. Figure 2.1 contains a chart of this approach.

The additional phases – plan, measure, optimize, and govern – are not shown in Figure 2.1 because the discover, define, design, and implement phases account for the majority of deliverables within a project. This approach provides a structure to organize tasks and deliverables in an easy-to-digest format.

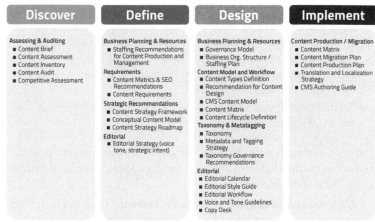

Discover	Define	Design	Implement
Assessing & Auditing ■ Content Brief ■ Content Assessment ■ Content Inventory ■ Content Audit ■ Competitive Assessment	**Business Planning & Resources** ■ Staffing Recommendations for Content Production and Management **Requirements** ■ Content Metrics & SEO Recommendations ■ Content Requirements **Strategic Recommendations** ■ Content Strategy Framework ■ Conceptual Content Model ■ Content Strategy Roadmap **Editorial** ■ Editorial Strategy (voice tone, strategic intent)	**Business Planning & Resources** ■ Governance Model ■ Business Org. Structure / Staffing Plan **Content Model and Workflow** ■ Content Types Definition ■ Recommendation for Content Design ■ CMS Content Model ■ Content Matrix ■ Content Lifecycle Definition **Taxonomy & Metatagging** ■ Taxonomy ■ Metadata and Tagging Strategy ■ Taxonomy Governance Recommendations **Editorial** ■ Editorial Calendar ■ Editorial Style Guide ■ Editorial Workflow ■ Voice and Tone Guidelines ■ Copy Desk	**Content Production / Migration** ■ Content Matrix ■ Content Migration Plan ■ Content Production Plan ■ Translation and Localization Strategy ■ CMS Authoring Guide

Copyright © 2014 Sapient Corporation

Figure 2.1 – SapientNitro project phases and enterprise-content deliverables

Using workshops to complete the project-definition focus areas

Workshops can help a team to complete exercises, such as defining the project's scope. As the enterprise content strategist, you may conduct several workshops with your content team or other stakeholders. Consider these best practices:

- Start with an agenda. Where applicable, use a slide presentation to facilitate the discussion. The agenda should include an objective or set of objectives for the session, for example: define the project's goal, objectives, scope, and purpose.
- Limit the workshop to two to four hours, allocating an appropriate amount of time for each objective and group session.
- Allow breaks every ninety minutes, and feed the participants. Supply coffee, tea, and water.
- Do exercises in teams. For example, one team may focus on defining what the project seeks to achieve, while another defines why. For an interesting scenario, give each team a different task, have them create a solution, then switch tasks with the other team and have them do the same. Once each team has completed both tasks, bring everyone together to compare.
- Create a straw document of how you think things should be and ask the group to discuss it.
- Set up exercises to gain closure on open issues.

- Use tools such as parking lots to capture issues or tangential discussions that might derail the workshop. A parking lot contains a list of issues or discussion points that a workshop cannot close, but which require attention at a later date. A project manager should capture issues as they come up, and then the facilitator should move on to keep the workshop on track.
- Set up ground rules, such as "silence does not equal consensus" and "don't beat a dead horse."

Have someone take notes, then review all decisions and next steps at the end of each session. Use workshops to finalize all project-definition focus areas. Include the following:

- **Objectives and requirements related to content:** For example, rolling out a new value proposition for the company, investing in SEO, bringing in an analytics engine, etc.
- **High-level technology requirements or constraints:** For example, system constraints on the content solution, requirements on localization and internationalization, and considerations related to vendors and other third-party entities and systems.
- **Publication requirements for each line of business:** Gather at a high level the content production volume for each group – how much content does each group produce and how much content has it already produced?

Once the team has successfully completed the project definition, work with a project manager to create a high-level plan. This plan may simply be the phases of the project mapped out with deliverables, similar to Figure 2.1, with some high-level timing for each phase. Although much of what the content team has completed here will remain the same throughout the project, the team should validate this work at the end of the assess and define phases, as validating will uncover more detailed requirements and a deeper understanding of the content ecosystem.

Additional reading

While this guide does not provide details about how to finalize a project's scope, information can be found in any guide to project management.

Project Management Institute maintains The Project Management Body of Knowledge,[1] the most widely recognized set of project management standards.

---

[1] http://www.pmi.org/PMBOK-Guide-and-Standards.aspx

CHAPTER 3
Assess Phase

The assess phase, sometimes referred to as the discovery phase or current-state analysis, provides a snapshot of an organization's content ecosystem. During this phase, you survey business goals, existing content, competitive content, content operations, content lifecycles, and governance structures. All this analysis provides a detailed understanding of how content performs and functions in the current environment. This understanding provides a foundation for an improved future-state model. By identifying gaps, issues, pain points, strengths, and requirements within the current state, the content strategist can determine how the content ecosystem functions within the organization – and how it needs to change.

In this chapter, you will learn the importance of the assess phase, understand how to conduct competitive and industry analysis, learn best practices for content inventories and audits, uncover the right way to conduct stakeholder interviews, and see the components of a stakeholder interview protocol.

Understanding the assess phase

As my friend and colleague Anne Casson notes, whoever does the assessment holds all the cards to the future content experience. A properly executed assess phase can provide a snapshot of the following:

- Business logic or rules for content intelligence
- Consumers or users who interact with the content
- Content lifecycle/production workflows
- Content organization, including taxonomies and metadata schemas
- Competitors' treatment of content
- Issues, gaps, and redundancies in content and production processes
- Social (user-generated) content efficacy
- Strengths, weaknesses, gaps, and issues with content governance
- Systems and integration points
- Accuracy, relevance, quality, timeliness, usability, and findability of content

These factors can greatly influence decisions for what to do in the future. But to effectively execute this effort, an enterprise content strategist must insist on sufficient time to guarantee a thorough assessment. Because it serves as the foundation for all future-state decisions and provides a blueprint from which to build a design, a light or quick-fix assess phase will prove detrimental to future design and implementation work, resulting in a compromised solution. At worst, it could result in a solution that does not meet the needs of content consumers at all.

Unfortunately, many organizations resist investing in a thorough assessment since they cannot always quantify its short-term value. To demonstrate that value, you may want to frame the solution around quick wins and longer-term initiatives. You can suggest that this phase, coupled with the define phase, will uncover a series of quick wins that will demonstrate value without a lengthy design or implementation effort.

Because this phase positions all future design decisions, you should spend enough time to understand each of these factors (quality of content, lifecycle, etc.). If you run this phase as part of a closed-loop process and choose to dig into only one or two content areas, then an abbreviated phase might work. For large organizations, plan for the assess phase to last eight to twelve weeks. For smaller organizations, four to six weeks may suffice. These timeframes depend on the availability of stakeholders and other variables.

Look at what needs to occur, and plan accordingly. Do not allow yourself to be pressured into underestimating this important effort. I have seen program managers push back on realistic estimates for this phase. If you give in to these demands, you may find yourself later blamed for agreeing to estimates you knew were unrealistic.

Performing stakeholder interviews

Successful stakeholder interviews provide an understanding of a current-state content ecosystem. Many of the concepts in this section require an understanding of the design principles and best practices outlined in Chapter 5, *Design Phase*. You conduct stakeholder interviews to uncover current-state business processes; validate the content inventory; and understand content scope, requirements, issues, gaps, and pain points.

Identifying stakeholders takes time, as does scheduling and coordinating interviews. Include authors, contributors, and other members from each line of business who handle content. Span the organizational matrix: junior, mid-level, and senior leaders. Include regional and global representatives. Get the content team's approval of the list of stakeholders.

You may want to conduct stakeholder interviews in conjunction with the competitive analysis and content-inventory exercises. Meet with each business unit and ascertain the types of content they handle. Ask interviewees what content most needs to be inventoried. Find out about their publication and production processes as well as any issues or gaps. Note any process or content redundancies. Consider showing interviewees a generic content lifecycle, such as the one in Figure 3.1.

When possible, meet with only one person or line of business at a time. In some cases, you might interview a group of people within a business unit. Ensure that someone takes notes. If you want to record the sessions, get agreement from the interviewee(s) and the organization.

Schedule two hours for each interview and send the protocol, or list of questions, before the meeting. Be sure to list any deliverables or examples that you would like the interviewee to bring. If you conduct this exercise remotely, set up a webshare so the interviewee can display file structures or CMS screens.

Use the following sample questions as a guide to create your interview protocol. I often send questions to the stakeholders in advance so they can think about answers or meet with their teams before the session. You can find the latest update of this stakeholder-interview protocol on my website.[1] (Note: in the protocol outlined below, "you" refers to the person whom you interview and "we/us" refers to you, the content strategist, the note taker, and anyone helps to facilitate.)

Business and project strategy

- What key organizational or business drivers, goals, and objectives should we consider?
- Why are we doing this work?
- What will constitute success?
- What long-term concerns should we address?
- What is the ideal solution or experience?
- Which constraints should we consider:
  - Budget: who controls or oversees the budgets for this work?
  - Timing: what are the target dates?
  - Technology: what changes might be needed?
- What are the challenges across stakeholders or lines of business, and are there conflicting interests?
- Who are the key executive stakeholders and sponsors?

---

[1] http://www.kevinpnichols.com/enterprise_content_strategy/

Content inventory and scope

- Do you have a list of all the types of content you work with?
- Is there a sitemap (for websites) or any information architecture work that we can leverage to determine the content types and scope?
- Have you performed any inventories or audits that we could leverage to determine the scope of the content we must consider?
- Can you help us create a comprehensive list of content types that your organization works with?
- How much content is there?
- What is the frequency and amount of content published to the site?
- Will any content be decommissioned in the near future? Do you plan to remove, delete, sunset, or archive any content?
- Are there licensing agreements in place that affect the use or decommissioning of content? (For content-migration efforts, you may have to review licensing agreements with the legal team.)
- Which content is syndicated or curated?
- What social channels do you use? How much content, and what content, do you produce for each?
- Do any laws or regulations require particular types of content?
- Do you have any content, editorial, or go-to-market calendars? If so, how often are they updated?
- How many new products are introduced annually, and what is the content production effort for this?
- If we begin this project, what are the content-critical dates we need to consider? Do you have go-to-market campaigns, new product launches, etc., that will occur mid-project? If so, will those elements need to be migrated into the new design?
- What content needs to be migrated? Has that content been audited to determine which must be migrated at launch and which can be migrated in later releases?
- How many lines within your business or organization should we consider? For example, what corporate content – annual reports, executive blogs, corporate-responsibility content, etc. – should be considered in addition to other consumer-facing content?

Production and publication processes

■ What are the major types of content in your organization? What are the unique content lifecycles associated with each?

> **Note:** A preliminary high-level inventory is useful in framing this question since content lifecycles are often tied to content types (for example, a warranty statement probably has a different workflow from a web banner to advertise a product).

■ Define your content publication lifecycle. Is the content lifecycle documented by production process workflows? If you do not have one documented, what are the high-level steps? Are the subprocesses within the primary flow documented? Who are the owners, content creators, reviewers, and approvers with each process, and what are the inputs and outputs of each?

■ Use Figure 3.1 as an example to help you capture areas related to each major component of the content lifecycle.

Figure 3.1 – Content lifecycle

■ What aspects of content acquisition, production, or delivery perform successfully in your group? What aspects have issues? What are your greatest pain points?

■ How do these kinds of content or processes add value to the organization? What does not add value?

- What are the larger issues that you face in terms of content acquisition, creation, management, production, delivery, and optimization?
- Who are the external stakeholders? Which internal stakeholders must we consider? Are there any vendors or third parties we should also consider? Do you have third-party content providers or do you syndicate content? This is what we know of thus far (list them). What are we missing?
- What cultural and institutional influences should we consider? What are the organizational politics? Do certain business units own or control how information is treated? What are the primary drivers behind information control?
- Could you help us construct the production process model for each additional content type, such as marketing messaging content, product-related content, or customer support content? What are the specific issues that you face in terms of content acquisition, creation, management, production, delivery, and optimization?
- Are there quality checklists in place for content review cycles?
- If content migration is required, is there a content migration strategy in place? Have you accounted for a global market rollout?
- What content outside the domain (microsites, campaigns, etc.) requires migration? Do Flash components or embedded applications require migration? Can these be migrated as-is, or do they require updated design or branding?
- Which channels (mobile, web, print, call center, etc.) do we need to consider? Among these channels, which content is derived from a single source and which is unique or differentiated per channel (for example, product specifications on the mobile site limited to four key specifications whereas the website provides all.)
- What is your archive process? Which laws or regulations are you bound to for archiving information? Which information must you preserve and for how long?

> **Note:** I keep internationalization/localization as a part of content production, but it will most definitely warrant a series of stakeholder interviews with each region or market. Because localization is a part of a larger content lifecycle, it is important to contextualize it within the larger model. The next set of questions deal with localization.

- Do you have a global presence? How many languages and countries should we consider for this work? Is any of your content localized? If so, what are your processes?
- Do you start with one language and one content source and then translate from that source?

- How do you ensure that content is messaged adequately for each region?
- Is the localization model decentralized?
- What issues and choke points do you encounter with localization?
- If we provide you with a content inventory, can you help us determine which content is globally shared versus locally differentiated?
- Do other regions know where and what they can differentiate? In other words, do they know what content they must support, what they can do with globally shared content, what they can create on their own, and which standards they must uphold when creating new content or localizing existing content?
- Do you have a model that supports the following, and are the business rules for each scenario clearly understood and adopted for the following?
  - ☐ Content that is distributed to regions where it can be localized
  - ☐ Content that localities can create and share either globally or with other localities
  - ☐ Content that is specific to a locale and not shared
- Are there issues with how localities or regions treat content? Do they ever go off-brand or create their own content in ways that do not comply with established rules?
- What unique content is produced for local markets?
- Do locales have budgets to support the amount of content required?
- Do locales work with translation services and vendors, and if so, what pain points exist within these processes?
- Do you experience issues in selling products or offering your services within certain markets?
- Is translation handled by third-party vendors, and if so, are those vendors familiar with your brand, style, voice, and tone guidelines? Do those vendors include translation for metadata and taxonomy values? Do they translate with SEO in mind?
- What metrics are in place to measure the efficacy of your localization strategy and approach, including sales data?

Technology

- Is there a CMS, DAM, or other content-related system in place today? If so, what is it? Are there additional systems to consider, such as a CRM system or product-catalog database?
- If there is a website, portal, or CMS, how is information organized within it today? Do data models or schemas exist that we can access?

- Do you leverage XML and metadata effectively for system integration and for externally facing code? Do you use XML to structure and identify content?
- What do you use for personalization?
- What types of analytics solutions do you have in place?
- Which other systems affect the content lifecycle?
- What channels, systems, or platforms should we consider (web, mobile, customer databases, CRM, analytics engines, etc.)?
- What are all the systems that affect content (for example, product catalogs or document management tools)? What are the strengths of these systems? What are the known issues with these systems? Are there gaps or integration issues?
- How do you manage your products today? Do you have a product hierarchy in place? Is this managed by a database or several databases? If so, identify and give a description of each. Could we have access to these schemas and/or hierarchies? How are products organized within this, and which elements do you capture?

Marketing strategy

- Is there a larger digital strategy that we need to be aware of to understand the digital landscape, its properties, and the content and brand requirements for the digital vision?
- Do you have a brand architecture in place? How is it documented, and are there any branding guidelines?
- What changes to your brand could affect our current project?
- Who are your competitors?
- In your opinion, what are the best-in-class websites/mobile (or whatever the content solution is) we should consider when determining how your site measures up?
- How many markets, regions, or locales do we need to consider in rolling out the content?
- Do you have a list of all current campaigns?
- Do you have a list of all future campaigns?
- What is your go-to-market (products to market) calendar?
- What social media platforms do you use?
- How many end-user distribution channels should we consider?
- What are your target audiences?
- What personas do you have based on behavioral characteristics of your end users or consumers?
- What types of search engine marketing do you have in place?

- How important is social media in your digital experience? How do you leverage it?
- What digital properties should be considered? What nondigital properties? Have you optimized experiences across all channels?

Analytics

- What are the key business goals and objectives we should consider? What key performance indicators do we need to understand?
- How do you capture user feedback regarding your content? How easy and quick is it to make updates based on the feedback? What applications cull data from customer-support call centers?
- What metrics measure your metadata, taxonomy, or search tools?
- What types of end-user feedback have you received regarding the ease of finding information within your platforms?
- What analytics tools do you use to measure access of your information and search queries used to find it?
- How do you test your content (A/B, multivariate, etc.)?
- What data do you have on your users?
- What types of web analytics do you collect?
- What levels of transparency exist for the end-user information you collect?
- Do you leverage metrics such as these for your digital experiences?
  - ☐ Length of visit within a specific channel or across channels
  - ☐ User paths or clickstream
  - ☐ Conversion metrics (purchase a product, download a white paper, sign up for a profile, register a product, apply for a job, etc.)
  - ☐ Bounce and exit rates
  - ☐ Depth of visit
  - ☐ Cost to convert
  - ☐ Visits to convert
  - ☐ Value of interaction
  - ☐ User interaction history
  - ☐ Social metrics such as share of voice and social listening
- What SEO strategies are in place for your website?
  - ☐ How do you do it?
  - ☐ Are analytics a component of it?
  - ☐ Which tools do you use?
  - ☐ Are authors trained on it?
  - ☐ How is it working?
- How mature is your SEO model?

- For web and mobile: Have you created a strategy to determine which pages you want to prioritize for SEO (home page, product landing page, corporate landing page, etc.)? Does every page have an SEO-optimized HTML page title, metadata keywords, and metadata descriptions? Are copywriters trained on the SEO process, including keywords they should be leveraging when they write? How much do you know about what your competitors use for labeling, SEO, or indexing information?
- Do you use Google analytics to identify keywords? If not, what tools do you use?
- Do you optimize your keywords based on mobile versus web?
- To what extent do your images have alt text, and to what extent do you use keywords in that alt text?
- Who creates the alt text for images, and when?
- Do you use smart URLs?
- Do you leverage social listening as an input to understanding what your consumers are saying about you, which content they share, and what they do or don't like about your business, products, or services?

Content structure, including metadata and taxonomy

- What taxonomies, thesauri, metadata structures, synonym rings, or other controlled vocabularies are in place in your organization? What software tools are used to manage the taxonomy or other controlled vocabularies? Do you have a listing of terms used to classify and identify your information from an end-user perspective?
- What metadata standards are in place? What tools are used to manage these standards?
- How do you currently categorize, label, and identify information in your organization? How many of these models exist?
- Do you use XML, for example DITA, to structure your documents? How well is your XML structure maintained? Which standards does it adhere to?
- What requirements exist to index and maintain content that is not in use? How is that content stored and indexed?
- If you have taxonomies in place, what do they accomplish (increase conversion on a website, standardize terms, organize information, drive personalization, decrease time spent trying to find information, integrate systems, etc.)?
- Who owns the taxonomies?
- What system do you use to tag content? What documentation exists? If none, is it needed? How well are the users of this system trained in the metadata standards and SEO methods?

■ What types of taxonomies do you use: back end? front end?[2] Consider that the person interviewed may need to understand the difference between a taxonomy and navigation scheme, a topic which is discussed in Chapter 5, *Design Phase*.

■ Do you have faceted or parametric navigation on your digital experience? If so, what technology enables and manages it? Do you update your facets based on user research and use, elevating facets that are used and sunsetting facets that are not? (Again, Chapter 5 will clarify faceted navigation.)

Content experience

The term *content experience* here refers to the future-state experience you are creating for your content consumers across all content types: editorial, messaging, branding, social, product, etc.

■ Does your organization enforce a content style guide or branding guide? What documentation exists?

■ Do you have voice and tone guidelines specific to channel, such as a web-content style guide?

■ Do you have a content brief in place?

■ What is your high-priority content?

■ What objectives must your content achieve?

> **Note:** Ask these questions for each content type and include high-profile pages such as the first two levels in a website, including a home page, landing pages, product-detail pages, and various section of a digital site.

■ What content is missing from your digital experience?

■ Which content opportunities are missing, such as personalization, cross-sell, social media integration, etc.?

■ How important is a rich content experience, such as multimedia or immersive and interactive content?

■ What are the strengths of your competitor's content experiences?

■ Do you create portable and/or shareable content? (This includes content that is widgetized and/or content that can be posted to social media or easily shared via email.)

■ Does your organization make investments in new content creation?

■ Do you produce thought leadership and if so, what? Who tracks and amplifies this activity? What thought leadership content is produced?

---

[2] An example of a back-end taxonomy is a product catalog in a product information database. An example of a front-end taxonomy is a product taxonomy used to generate faceted navigation and tagging on a website.

- What is your customer lifecycle when you are deciding what new content to create and how to otherwise enhance people's experience of your content?

> **Note:** The customer journey includes not just the sales or purchasing funnel but also content a customer would use after he or she has purchased a product, such as support content, warranty or service updates, product updates, or content to enhance the customer's relationship with the brand.

- What intelligence is built into your content?
  - ☐ How do you personalize content?
  - ☐ How do you up-sell, cross-sell, or use CRM to target content?
  - ☐ How do you use recommendation engines on your website?
  - ☐ How do you vary the states at which a user can access content? What are the current "flavors" of content?[3] Are there documented decision trees concerning user access to content?
- For the new solution/design, which content must be kept? (This question may require validation of the content inventory and may be more suitable to ask when validating the inventory.)

Omnichannel and multichannel strategy

See Chapter 5 for clarification on omnichannel, responsive, adaptive, and other concepts covered within these questions.

- Do you have multiple channels to which you publish content? If so, what are they?
- Do you optimize content per each channel (for example, unique content for mobile smartphone and desktop website)?
- Do you have an omnichannel strategy in place? If so, is your strategy documented?
- What challenges do you face with multichannel publishing?
- Do you have a mobile strategy that considers smartphone, tablet, and feature phones? Do any of your consumers live in countries where feature phones are primarily used?
- Do you use customer journeys and user tasks across multiple channels to identify which content to deliver to each channel to support a unified experience? For example, to purchase a product, a consumer might go from a TV ad to a tablet (look up the company) to a desktop website (to do further research) to a mobile device (to locate a store or scan a QR code in the store) and expect in-store content from a

---

[3] By flavor we mean an instance of content targeted to a specific user segment or persona or targeted to a specific customer journey or user preference.

sales representative to support the experience. The consumer may share his or her overall experience on social networks or expect a personalized experience when dealing with customer support.

■ Do you have metrics and analytics in place to measure content performance in all channels?

■ Do you optimize content based upon analytics and metrics within each channel?

■ For mobile devices, do you leverage responsive or adaptive design or a hybrid model? Do you understand the differences?

■ What unique content do you have in each channel and what content do you share across channels?

Governance

■ Is there a governance model in place for content?
  □ For digital governance overall?
  □ For content governance?
  □ For taxonomy and metadata?

■ Are there issues with governance – either lack of governance or dysfunction within the model?

■ Which elements of governance are federated versus which are centralized, decentralized, or centralized with federated aspects?

■ What types of governance are enforced by standards such as editorial and brand guidelines?

■ How does the governance structure function, and who is responsible for its development and enforcement?

■ What roles exist within your governance structure?

■ Is there a governance charter? How often does the governance team meet? Who is involved with it?

■ If the governance does not exist by committee, does it exist in the format of standards or regulations?

Entitlements

■ Are there entitlements (that is, is access limited to certain types of content)? How many entitlements exist? Are there sign-off controls? What are the touchpoints?

■ Do you have login information for any sites that require authentication?

■ Who will need access to any new content systems, and what will they do with those systems? Which types of user roles and entitlements do you envision? Do you have a current list of each with your current content systems?

Conducting a content inventory and audit

Conduct a content inventory and audit at the beginning of the assess phase, which you can do in conjunction with stakeholder interviews. A content inventory answers the question: What content, and how much content, do I have? An audit answers the question: Does that content meet my and my users' (customers, end-users, consumers, etc) needs?

Here's another way to say it: inventories are quantitative and audits are qualitative. Some content strategists prefer to inventory first and then audit. On enterprise content strategy projects, I find it preferable to do both simultaneously.

Future content designs might change the way content quality and relevance are viewed. So the audit might require further validation at a later date. Begin a project requiring content migration only after completing an inventory and audit. Both will inform the volume and scope of content to be migrated.

The inventory will uncover all the content, whereas the audit will indicate the content quality and whether it should be migrated as is, reworked, or deleted entirely. For closed-loop projects where audits are conducted semiannually or as part of an ongoing cycle, the approaches outlined below still apply.

For enterprise efforts, before executing this work, agree on the scope of content to assess. For example, a large-scale enterprise content inventory and audit may include the following areas:

- Desktop websites, including microsites
- Mobile websites and apps, including those for tablets, smartphones, and feature phones (each channel may require separate inventories and audits)
- Product packaging
- Social and user-generated content
- Customer call center or support content
- Product content, such as user guides and instruction manuals
- Internal organization content, such as that found in employee portals
- Legal, regulatory, and compliance content
- HR content for internal organizations
- Publications not covered in the above categories

You may require more than one individual or team to complete each area. Sometimes I have seen these efforts conducted by each line of business or owners in parallel.

To do a proper audit, first establish the criteria you are auditing against. Factor in the project or business goals, and define the following:

- What do we want to achieve?
- Are there existing analytics or metrics related to content performance? Are we meeting our existing objectives?
- What constitutes success and good content?

You may turn to the project goals, objectives, or any other performance criteria used to evaluate content to answer these questions. After you establish criteria, ensure that others on the content team agree with the approach. Then begin the inventory and audit.

In most cases, you will not capture a comprehensive list of content pieces, although content migration efforts might require such an approach. Thus, you probably will not need to capture every press release. You should at least note the approximate number of each type of article, say, about a thousand press releases. For projects requiring migration, you may need to inventory every page within the experience.

For a thorough inventory and audit, review all the content within the current-state scope, and create a spreadsheet where you can sort and group the information. Survey the website, CMS, or internal systems, and list all the major content types. As you do so, list the various levels under each type. Keep this list hierarchical within the spreadsheet so the content is displayed in context. For example, on a website it might be:

```
Corporate Information → Investor Relation → Annual Report
```

To automate some of the most time-consuming parts of the process, you can use a tool like the Content Analysis Tool (CAT).[4] Using such a tool, you can extract a preliminary content inventory and audit upon which you can build. See the next section, "Content inventory and audit: fields to capture," for a description of how to conduct a manual process. This approach also works well if you are using a tool such as CAT.

---

[4] http://www.content-insight.com/

Content inventory and audit: fields to capture

In your inventory and audit, you may want to capture the information listed below. You can download a sample template[5] that uses these fields from my website. Use the template as a starting point, and amend it based on your project needs.

Content volume and scope section

- ■ **ID #:** Assign a unique ID to each piece of content. If applicable, use a numbering or labeling system that could be employed in the future-state design.

- ■ **Document owner:** Identify the owner of the document, which in some cases may be a business unit.

- ■ **Document title or topic:** Define the primary themes that make up the content. You can use the name of the document, section, or HTML page for this purpose (for example, Press Release, Careers, Home page, etc.) It is important to capture each topic or type of content represented on the site or within the system, but it is often unnecessary to capture each piece of content. For example, there may be hundreds of press releases. The number can be captured in the volume field, whereas the type of content – press release – need be captured only once.

- ■ **Level 2 subtopic (levels 2–X):** Identify the subtopics included in the document or page. This is especially necessary for an enterprise project that evaluates one large document, such as a product plan. Subtopics can be obtained from a table of contents, content object, or asset library.

- ■ **Content type:** Capture the nature of the document. A sample list of *content types* include form pages on a website, user guides for products, home pages, legal disclaimers, product landing pages, help or FAQ pages, news, warranty statements, press releases, corporate biographies, annual reports, etc.

- ■ **Notable functionality:** Convey critical functionality as it relates to the content within the site or system. For example, on a website this might be navigation, search, RSS feeds, user-generated content, etc.

- ■ **Description:** Describe what the content is, its primary theme, and why it was created. For some efforts, this may not be necessary if the same content strategist remains on the project throughout its duration. For websites, you can sometimes copy the metadata description for this purpose. If you do, verify that the description is accurate.

- ■ **URLs:** Some projects require URLs for every asset or page. Others require representative URLs. It is not necessary in most cases to list

---

[5] http://kevinpnichols.com/downloads/kpn_content_audit.xls

every URL per content type (for example, do not list each individual press release).

■ **Volume:** Note the total number of documents that exist for each content type. For example, note that there are 57 corporate bios. It is imperative to track quantity because this data informs the production plan and overall scope of the project.

Metadata and SEO section

■ **HTML page title:** This will appear at the top of the browser window.

■ **Meta description:** This is important from a search marketing perspective. This short, keyword-rich paragraph in the code of the page will often show up in search results along with a link to the found content. A clear description could play an important role in compelling users to click through.

■ **Meta keywords:** Some search engines index and use keywords along with other factors to determine the ranking of a page. Keywords are relevant terms that describe your content.

Additional inventory aspects section

■ **Doc format:** Note the document format: HTML, JPG, GIF, PDF, XLS, DOC, MPEG, etc.

■ **Author:** If the author is known, note who created the content. This can be a line of business rather than an individual contributor (for example, marketing, product development, etc.). If this is not known, ask the content team to provide the data.

■ **Last updated or published:** Capture how often the content is updated: daily, weekly, monthly, yearly, never, and unknown. If this column is irrelevant, you may need a date column to note when the content was last published.

■ **Update frequency:** Note how frequently the content requires an update. This is important for sites or portals that need updated content to ensure their integrity, such as a message from a CEO or a module that has a refresh rate.

■ **CMS template:** Record the name of the page template in the CMS that should be used to build this page.

Business rules for intelligent content section

■ **Audience:** Note who will consume or use the content or who is the desired recipient. If you target segments and these are known, capture each. This could be a targeted persona or user journey. You may need separate columns for persona, segment, and journey.

- **Instances/variations:** Note if there are several variations of the same type of content. This is particularly useful if content is personalized for an authenticated or targeted consumer. This field captures any type of content that is generated based on business rules or decision trees, for example, content meant for an authenticated audience.

- **Rules for use:** Note any additional rules for the content's use or reuse: where, when, and why can the content be used? Also, note any rules related to personalization, such as what content is displayed for an authenticated user versus a non-authenticated user.

- **Channel:** What is the target channel for the content, such as mobile smartphone, feature phone, or in-store kiosk.

Qualitative assessment section

- **High, medium, low:** Indicate the priority of the content with these three columns. High means that the content is absolutely necessary. Medium means that it is important but not absolutely necessary. Low means that it is not necessary and is of little importance. Place an X in the appropriate column.

- **Redundancy:** If the content is redundant, list instances.

- **Quality:** Create a prioritization scheme for the quality of the content: E (Excellent), G (Good), S (Satisfactory), or P (Poor). In making this determination, consider whether the content is up to date, whether it's on message, and whether it meets its performance criteria.

- **M/D/R:** Note if the content will be migrated (M), deleted (D), or revised (R). This analysis should also be weighed against the quality assessment and validated by the content team. Even if the content is necessary for the future-state design, it may prove better to create it from scratch.

- **Issues:** Capture any additional issues, such as gaps in content.

- **Rating:** Use a number scale to weigh the content vis-à-vis the evaluation criteria; does the content meet the desired performance?

Document and channel input/outputs section

- **Inputs/sources (system):** Define the system inputs for the content (that is, which systems feed the content), and identify sources for syndicated or third-party content.

- **Outputs (channel):** List which systems content is fed to and where content is published, offline as well as online. This information is especially important in multichannel environments.

- **Inputs/sources (document):** Define the inputs necessary to complete the document or information (marketing plan, product-development spec sheet, etc.).

- **Outputs (document):** List other documents that are fed by the content. This information is especially useful if an inventory is necessary for objects that feed dynamic content.

> **Caution:** Do not use a spider or inventory application without manually verifying the results. Applications may not capture all the content. They certainly can't audit the content for quality the way a seasoned practitioner can.

When used properly, a spider or a tool such as CAT can help ensure that you don't miss content. These tools can also identify content that search engines do not index. If you use an automated tool, make sure you verify what the tool fails to index. This information shows you which content search crawlers fail to index and, thus, reveals important details about the findability of the content and its performance in search engine optimization. If an inventory tool does not find certain pages, most likely the content will not be indexed by search engines.

After you finish the inventory, have the content team ensure that all necessary lines of business (especially those who own content within it) validate the inventory. You should not move forward with additional content work until the content team signs off on this document, and sign-off means that the inventory and audit capture all content within the current state. In other words, all content owners must sign off on the inventory as capturing and properly inventorying all of their content.

I have witnessed projects with Fortune 100 companies where an inventory failed to account for major content areas, and project teams discovered this content too late. As a result, the companies were forced to delay website launches significantly because existing content that was not accounted for was needed before the future-state experience could launch. And since the experience design failed to provide a place for this content, the functional and interactive designs required rework.

Another important consideration: content does not just mean text; it means all assets, including images, videos, and PDFs as well as all metadata associated with each content type.

Each content stakeholder and line of business should validate that the following are adequately represented in the inventory:

- All types of content within the line of business
- Each content type in priority order
- All inputs or outputs for each content type: What is required to create the content? What are the outputs or deliverables?

- Any types of content that are missing or are known to be forthcoming (for example, a future campaign or a new product launch)
- Authors and sources for content

A word of caution here. For projects that migrate content, make it clear that sign-off covers the entire scope of content necessary for migration. Don't begin a content migration until you have a complete inventory of all current-state content signed off by every team that owns content. Also capture any planned content releases, editorial calendars, and campaigns.

Completing competitive and industry analyses

When considering external-facing content, you should recognize competitive analysis as one of your best friends for differentiating your content and ensuring that your content experience contains everything it should. Looking at what competitors do, how they do it, and what they say can help you identify opportunities and see what they are doing better than you. If you know who your competitors are, then you should continuously review what they are doing and how they are doing it.

If you are a nonprofit organization or if you feel you have no direct competitors, then looking at the content offered by similar organizations can provide you with opportunities to improve your experience. Build this approach into a semi-annual or annual audit. A tool such as a content inventory or audit of competitive or related websites can help you uncover features, functionality, and positioning that your competition uses. No matter the size of your business or organization, you should review trends and related organizations to determine opportunities for your future content priorities.

Research should survey how competitor sites and applications categorize and treat information and the channels and methods they use to communicate information. These may include mobile platforms, websites, microsites, and social networking sites such as Facebook and Twitter.

For external websites, analyze how the site treats the home, landing, section, and article pages. Your analysis should answer the following questions:

- Do home pages show a variety of products, services, or offerings, and do they tell the story of the brand?
- Is the right content (based on audience insights and research) integrated within category and product-listing pages?

■ How are social-engagement opportunities (user-generated content via social media, such as Pinterest) integrated into the experience?

■ How is video used to communicate about products, user instructions, and brands?

In addition, analyze the way competitors treat metadata and keywords. Review where keyword searches are effective and not effective. Which keyword searches yield which results?

For an internal project, on a portal for example, analyst reports and whitepapers will help you identify issues and considerations. Many portal technologies have online design and development documentation available. Search online for the latest usability reports for portals. These reports usually include examples of top sites, winners of contests, or those that score high on usability.

You can search by topic such as corporate social responsibility (CSR), retail, or mobile to capture what is new and who has written a report. Many reports are free. Look for them in press releases, but expect to do some digging to find them.

Here are some free resources that provide information on trends and content performance:

■ **Alexa:** Web analytics and benchmarking data (alexa.com)

■ **Nielsen press releases:** White papers about technology and media trends (nielsen.com/us/en/reports.html)

■ **Nielsen Norman Group reports:** Reports on various areas of user experience (nngroup.com/reports/)

■ **Our Mobile Planet:** Smartphone and adoption data on forty-eight countries (thinkwithgoogle.com/mobileplanet/en/[9])

■ **Pew Internet:** Reports on shifting American behavior as it pertains to the internet (pewinternet.org)

■ **Comscore press releases:** White papers about technology and media trends (comscore.com/Insights/Press-Releases/(offset)/10)

■ **Google insights:** Range of topics, from user behavior on screen size to trends in technology (thinkwithgoogle.com)

Forrester (forrester.com) and Gartner (gartner.com) also offer reports, but these reports are not free.

Regardless of the size of your company or organization, empower yourself with knowledge of trends in the use of external-facing content.

---

[9] http://think.withgoogle.com/mobileplanet/en/

This information can help you decide what to do and why. For internal content, evaluating the way others handle the content can help you shape a robust and refined model.

Engage the content team in the assessment

For large organizations, you may want to conduct all of the activities described above – inventories, audits, and stakeholder interviews – simultaneously. You can use workshops to collect stakeholder requirements, such as an analytics workshop with members of the analytics team or a content lifecycle workshop with key people who have roles in content publishing. Workshops can help you gain information you need and – if you include all the necessary stakeholders – can help you reach alignment on issues, gaps, and opportunities in each group.

Another approach you might find effective is to create a worksheet in a spreadsheet for the content team and each line of business that creates content. Have each group document its content lifecycles. This approach requires that you conduct two workshops. In the first workshop, you take the group through the process of capturing their content lifecycles. They should answer key questions identified in the above protocol, such as issues, gaps, redundancies, and pain points. They should capture their end-to-end lifecycle processes as well. After you receive this input from all the necessary stakeholders, you can document the lifecycles visually, perhaps using a tool like Visio and identify the issues within each. In the second workshop, you review and validate your work. See Chapter 5 for more on documenting and creating content lifecycles.

For all major work in this phase, including audit and inventory, validate your final deliverables with the content team. Vet each version of the process flow and content-audit findings. Ensure that the entire team reviews the final documents for any issues. They should assess the final product as a whole and review each component.

Additional reading

For more on content discovery and current-state assessment, see Paula Ladenburg Land's *Content Audits and Inventories: A Handbook*[12].

CHAPTER 4
Define Phase

The define phase is your opportunity to set the stage for your future digital and offline content experiences. In the define phase, you define the future content experience based on what you learned in the assess phase. As you sift through the findings of the assess phase, you will most likely identify issues that warrant a response. As you assimilate your findings, tie any issue or gap either to an implication (the impact on the success or efficacy of a solution or experience) or to a recommendation for future improvements. Take the issues, gaps, and strengths you identified and create a vision of how these will manifest in a successful design, thus developing your roadmap for the overall content experience and ecosystem.

This chapter covers how to create a content strategy framework, write audit findings, and construct a content strategy roadmap. For content migration projects, you may need a migration strategy. For projects with *personalization* or omnichannel considerations, you may need personalization and omnichannel strategies.

Creating a content strategy framework

A content strategy framework takes the learnings from the audit, the business objectives and goals, and any other inputs from the assess phase to frame a recommendation for the future-state experience. The framework document captures gaps, issues, and opportunities within the current ecosystem and presents recommendations. In some cases, you may wish to create separate documents for the audit report and the strategic recommendations. However, a comprehensive document may serve you better since it tells a more holistic story, presenting a narrative of where the content ecosystem should evolve.

The framework document includes three primary components:

- **Content findings and implications (audit report):** Reports the findings in the audit with implications for each.
- **Framework and strategic recommendations:** Describes how the ecosystem should advance.
- **Roadmaps:** Shows short-term, near-term, and long-term focus areas, such as what should happen for a new launch or design and where and how it should mature over time.

To complete this document, you review the business goals and objectives, content inventory and audit, stakeholder interviews, competitive information, content lifecycle analysis, and governance models. From these, you extract current issues, gaps, choke points, and redundancies. This information will inform the areas the future-state design must address. Highlight all recommendations that can be done easily and quickly, such as process adjustments that involve no system updates and minimal cost while delivering immediate value.

Sample sections in a framework document

Your framework document needs several sections, including some or all of those listed here:

Section	Description
Introduction	State the scope of the audit, what it covers, and why it was completed.
Approach	Explain the approach you used in the assess phase to arrive at the findings and recommendations. For example: ■ Review of the business goals and objectives ■ Stakeholder interviews (list the sessions) ■ Workshops (list the sessions) ■ Archetypes based on research ■ Site inventory and audit of all content and channels, including social, and the audit-criteria used.
Business goals and objectives	List any business goals and objectives, including project goals and objectives critical to the content efforts.

Audit findings and implications	Divide the audit findings and implications into the following subsections:
	1. **Business, marketing, and consumer goals and objectives:**
	  a. Are the goals and objectives being met from a business perspective?
	  b. Who are the target consumers, and has our organization optimized content for each based on persona, segment, and consumer/user journeys?
	  c. Are the marketing and sales goals and objectives being met? For example, does the content generate the expected sales?

2. **Content quality:**
   a. Are the objectives of the content achieved? Can a consumer accomplish all desired tasks?
   b. Is the content on-brand and consistent throughout the experience?
   c. Is the content up-to-date, accurate, and relevant for every channel and experience?
   d. Is the content effective? Does it embody a rich experience leveraging syndicated, social, and rich media when relevant?
   e. How well does content perform in each channel and across channels? Can a content consumer accomplish the necessary tasks within each channel or, for omnichannel experiences, with effective navigation?

3. **Content structure and priorities:**
   a. Does the content structure support the goals, objectives, and priorities of the content?
   b. Is navigation intuitive and consumer friendly?
   c. Is search supported by a robust taxonomy, and do results return meaningful content?

4. **Accessibility compliance:** Is the content accessible for people with disabilities? For more on this topic, see the W3C Web Accessibility Initiative.[1] The W3C also maintains a list of web accessibility evaluation tools.[2] Include the results of any accessibility testing in the audit report.

5. **Content lifecycle:** How does the organization acquire, create, review, maintain, publish, localize, evaluate, and optimize content? What about curation or syndication? Identify every lifecycle.

6. **Content analytics:** How does content perform overall? See Chapter 7 for a complete list of metrics related to content performance.

7. **SEO, taxonomy and metadata:**
   a. How strongly does SEO perform in the digital properties?
   b. Does the taxonomy support search, personalization, recommendations, and semantic and

---

[1] http://www.w3.org/WAI/intro/accessibility.php
[2] http://www.w3.org/WAI/ER/tools/complete

intelligent content (if applicable) such as cross-sell/up-sell and predictive search?

c. How effective is the metadata?

8. **Content governance:** Do the operational processes, tools, standards, and governance policies support ongoing content maintenance and evolution?

Framework with strategic recommendations

Describe the future-state framework. Potential subsections:

■ **Business, marketing, and consumer (or user) goals:** What needs to happen to meet the goals of the business, marketing, and consumers?

■ **Content experience:** What are the recommendations for the consumer content experience? List all required and recommended content types with definitions for each. Chapter 5 shows how to identify content types.

■ **Multimedia and social media:** What social considerations require improvement for the content experience and business objectives?

■ **Personalization:** If personalizing content, such as for an e-commerce website, what do you recommend for the strategic approach and roadmap?

■ **Content lifecycle:** What are the lifecycle pain points per content type and distribution point, and how can these be resolved?

■ **Content governance:** What are the governance issues and recommendations?

■ **Search engine optimization and taxonomy:** For consumer-facing websites, how does search perform both onsite (internal search on a portal, website, or application) and in organic results?

■ **Analytics:** What is the analytics strategy, and what can be done better?

Roadmaps

Articulate what happens from the initial improvements through to a fully realized state. You may have more than one roadmap. Examples:

■ Content experience
■ Content lifecycles
■ Personalization
■ Content governance

Writing audit findings and implications

Analyzing and summarizing the audit findings may take several weeks. In this process, you not only identify the current ecosystem's issues, gaps, opportunities, and strengths, but you also evaluate the ecosystem and draw conclusions.

As you undertake this process, remember this insightful axiom from Twitter co-founder Biz Stone:

> Positive culture comes from being mindful,
> and respecting your coworkers, and being empathetic.
> —Biz Stone, co-founder, Twitter

I have seen audits presented in a format that illuminates only the pain points. Such an approach can offend stakeholders or those involved with the work, making them feel as if they have to defend their work. I have also seen audits that use terms like "horrible," "ugly," and "completely unusable." Not even the most patient website owner or product-line content producer wants to sit through a meeting where he or she hears a long list of things that you found wrong. These folks may feel exposed or called out, and they may resent being involved in the effort.

Often, issues that you find were not entirely conceived out of choice. In many cases, those involved with the work already know what could be improved. So be mindful and respectful of the work that has been evaluated, even if significant issues exist. Use value-neutral terms, and stick to the ways that the issue prevents an organization from meeting business objectives or affects consumer tasks (such as an inability to easily find and purchase a product). As I uncover areas for improvement, I often acknowledge each line of business responsible for various areas of the content ecosystem and the challenges or constraints they face, praising what they achieved within the current system.

When creating your framework document, include appropriate sections, such as those listed in the section titled "Sample sections in a framework document" (p. 50). Work through each area by listing the key findings. An audit report should call attention to key themes – as opposed to listing each issue – and then provide a few examples.

For example, if you find that a website's images lack alt text and that the page structure impedes accessibility, your finding may look like this:

- **Marketing goal:** Reach the maximum number of consumers and potential consumers with rich, relevant, timely content.
- **Finding:** The website does not support accessibility.
- **Examples:** Images on the home page, landing pages, and product pages lack alt text. Pages lack a structure to support accessibility.
- **Implication:** The site prevents people with disabilities such as visual impairment from using the site effectively.

Notice that the goal sets up the finding and implication to a desired benchmark. Chapter 8, *Optimize Phase*, discusses ways to identify goals and objectives for your content ecosystem.

You may be wondering, "What about all the details I captured in the audit spreadsheet?" Don't worry, you will use those details when fixing issues in the future-state. In fact, you may want to address some easy-to-fix issues – like creating alt text for images – immediately following the define phase. When writing up your findings, though, simply refer to the content-audit document as the place where those details were captured.

Table 4.1 shows an example of what might go into the "Audit findings and implications" section of a content strategy framework for a website.

Table 4.1 – Example of a website audit table of contents

Focus area	Description
Home page	Given the high priority nature of this page, break down the page into its primary components and address each area. For example, the rotating carousel on the home page does not feature any videos, important textual copy is embedded in the images, and content owners rarely update their content on the homepage.
Product-category landing pages	A category page in this instance might be Women's Clothes. There may be several levels of category pages, such as Women's Clothes > Dresses >Skirts. Follow the same approach as the home page. Address each level.
Product landing pages	Look at this as a page type and address the primary themes that the audit uncovers.
User-generated content	You may want this as its own section, or you may address these areas within the page types where these are embedded. For example, user ratings, reviews, or comments may be embedded in a variety of pages.

Focus area	Description
Social media	These may include an audit of the actual social properties, and you may break it into subsections based on each social site (Facebook, Twitter, Pinterest, etc.).
User profile	Address each area of the user profile.
Corporate pages	You may break these into subcategories such as investor relations, news and events, careers, about us, corporate responsibility, etc.
Tools	Look at any tools within the experience. Examples: product-comparison tool, mortgage calculator.
Shopping cart	Include the end-to-end experience of adding items to a cart, purchasing, and checking out.
Campaign pages or banners	Review any marketing campaign areas, including any microsites.
Legal, copyright, and privacy pages	These areas, often found in the footer of a website, are also important to feature in the audit report.

For larger enterprise audits, you may survey other areas. Examples:

- Desktop websites
- Mobile websites and apps, including those for tablets, smartphones, and feature phones
- Microsites
- Multiple regional or local websites for international efforts
- Product packaging
- Customer call center or support content
- Product content, such as user guides
- Internal organization content, such as that found within employee portals
- Legal, regulatory, and compliance content
- User-generated content and social media
- HR content for internal organizations

After you have this section of the framework complete, vet your audit findings with the content team. You will want them to buy into the key themes uncovered before you draft the strategic recommendations because the audit will inform that effort.

Creating the framework and strategic recommendations

The framework and strategic recommendations tell a critical story of how the content ecosystem should evolve. In this phase of work, you do not yet design future-state solutions. Rather, you address what the design phase should consider by answering this question: which solutions or content are necessary to meet the business and organization goals and to enhance the relationship between the organization and the consumer?

At this point in creating the framework, list primary themes from the assess phase. Explore each area of the ecosystem; identify the key issues, gaps, and redundancies in the current state; and tie each to a specific recommendation. For example, if you have a section on accessibility within the framework, you might want to define accessibility, explain the importance of the business and consumer goals and objectives, and identify places where a lack of accessibility requires attention.

Recommendation: Create meaningful and relevant alt text for all images on the website. Include this work in the scope for future content creation, and create a workflow for this textual creation process that leverages SEO expertise as well. This will help the site comply with accessibility standards and increase the effectiveness of SEO, further expanding the brand's reach to new consumers.

> Often, these recommendations become future projects.

While you finalize this document, vet the audit report with the content team and major stakeholders to ensure their buy-in. Then, take key stakeholders through the framework document. Once you and the content team finish, go back to your original plan to prioritize and modify as necessary. The planning documents may change significantly from the earlier stages. Set expectations during the plan phase that the design scope cannot be locked down until you complete the define phase.

Designing a roadmap

A roadmap identifies both long-term and short-term projects that map to the initial project's goals. For enterprise content strategy engagements, a roadmap proves useful because generally more than one project makes up the overall initiative. To complete this work, revisit the plan phase to ensure that all projects, objectives, and goals are understood. However, the assess phase and the analysis of that work in the define phase may uncover additional projects or may reprioritize the work. There are many types of roadmaps you could create. This guide will show two types, one which shows high-level projects and focus areas over a three-year span and a more specific roadmap for omnichannel personalization. Table 4.2 presents a roadmap for an enterprise engagement.

Table 4.2 – Three-year enterprise content strategy roadmap

2014	2015	2016
Project goal: Fully optimize the content ecosystem within a three-year period to support all channels within the consumer experience.		
Kick off identified projects and launch	**Evolve the ecosystem**	**Continual enrichment**
Technology projects	**Technology projects**	**Governance**
Website redesign with new content management system (CMS)	Optimize each technology area from learnings uncovered in phase 1	Identify new projects based on business goals and objectives, new technology, and learnings from ongoing analytics
Digital asset management integration with new CMS	Integrate customer relationship management tool with publishing tools	
Optimize for mobile smartphone, desktop website, and feature phone; use best practices for adaptive design	Expand publishing to offline materials through system integration	
Content experience	**Content experience**	
Improve editorial calendar and create a monthly update process based on analytics and business inputs	Evolve content experience to support offline channels	
Create content to support each digital channel	Roll out phase 2 of personalization based on learnings from phase 1	
Begin personalization strategy with first phase of personalization in all digital channels	Create more immersive experiences with further investment in video and online tools	
Identify providers for syndicated content to support trends content targeted to specific personas		
Create an enterprise taxonomy to support the overall experience		

2014	2015	2016
Analytics	**Analytics**	
Expand *analytics* strategy to cover all areas of consumer-facing content Identify analytics to measure internal performance of content lifecycle and publishing processes	Determine costs saved through efficiencies gained and process improvements Determine content-experience-optimization areas	
Governance	**Governance**	
Create an optimized *governance* structure to support the ecosystem Update governance scope, team structure, and charter	Leverage governance for the strategic direction for the entire content ecosystem	

Notice in Table 4.2 how the roadmap contains an overall goal with phases that plot specific projects and focus areas. Table 4.3 provides example of a roadmap, with an omnichannel focus.

Finalizing the define phase

After you complete all these activities, revisit your original plans identified in plan phase. Work with a project manager and project team to refine those plans and create a detailed project plan for the design phase. A business analyst can document requirements and incorporate these into a project plan, within which a project manager can properly identify tasks with timing, resources, and dependencies.

In many cases, you may require additional meetings with executive stakeholders to secure sign off for your proposed efforts. A define phase must incorporate the final design plan before the design phase can be kicked off. You may have other dependencies, such as technology and user experience teams within the overall design plan. Upon finalizing the plan, we kick off the next phase of work: the design phase.

Table 4.3 – Omnichannel personalization roadmap

Launch	9–12 months post launch	18+ months post launch
Foundation	**Evolution**	**Enrichment**
1. Identify initial personas and segments to target per channel. 2. Establish the content needed to support each group (what do we want to serve up to each segment and persona and to what degree?). 3. Establish the rules for serving up content (if User X indicates he or she is Y in user profile, then serve up this content…) per channel per user task. 4. Account for taxonomy and controlled vocabularies to enable the experience. 5. Develop all necessary content to support each personalization instance proposed. 6. Roll out personalization based on foundational criteria. 7. Ensure proper metrics to track consumer interaction and behaviors so these can be examined for future optimization.	1. Test existing content by running ongoing metrics and audits to see how consumers interact with the content experience. 2. Identify additional content areas, such as enhanced cross-sell, up-sell. 3. Test assumed customer journeys across channels to verify accuracy and optimize content performance. 4. Roll out enhanced personalization per channel.	1. Integrate omnichannel in all channels. 2. Continue to create immersive content. 3. Leverage new or emerging technologies and techniques. 4. Optimize per business needs, analytics, and consumer trends.

Additional reading

For a thorough assessment of the content discovery and current-state assessment approach, see Paula Ladenburg Land's *Content Audits and Inventories: A Handbook*[12].

CHAPTER 5
Design Phase

GOVERN

4. Design

Once you complete the plan, assess, and define phases, you are ready to embark on one of the most exciting phases of enterprise content strategy work: the design phase.

All your previous efforts culminate in this phase, evolving that work into a desired model.

During the design phase, you design several pieces of the content ecosystem, including these:

- Strategic intent for content experience
- Content lifecycles
- Content types
- Taxonomy and metadata
- Content logic in content experience
- Content modeling, including all rules for content
- Page-level content strategy
- Editorial guidelines, including voice and tone definition

This chapter will cover best practices for designing and developing these pieces, include step-by-step instructions for each.

Creating a strategic intent for content experience

All content experiences should start with a strategic intent. A strategic intent answers these questions:

- Who is the audience for the content?
- Which business goal and objectives will the content fulfill?
- What consumer objectives or needs should we meet?
- In which channels should the content reside?
- When is the content required?

The define phase will have uncovered the answers to these questions. In fact, in many cases you should complete the bulk of this effort in the define phase. However, during define phase, you may encounter additional projects or discover that you lack the information necessary to inform the strategic approach.

To create a strategic intent, start with a *content brief*, creative brief, competitive analysis, current-state findings, heuristic analysis, and any other material you need to define the objectives for the content. Review the content audit to determine the shortcomings and strengths of your content's current state. For new experiences, such as a new website where no current content exists or an experience overhaul where you must start from scratch, use competitive data and user research to determine content priorities.

While you undergo this effort, schedule regular design sessions with an information architect on the project team. You should have a high-level architecture or site map for digital interface solutions. This will provide a structure for how content surfaces within the digital experience. When you finalize this work, document your findings. This document answers questions about overall experience and clearly states the objectives and editorial goals. You should verify that this information ties back to the business objectives of the project.

A strategic intent for a website contains the following:

- Mission of the site or experience
- Objectives the site or experience must achieve
- Audience (targeted consumers) and channels
- Types of content necessary to support the experience and objectives
- Prioritization of that content

Do not begin other design-phase activities until you finalize the strategic intent around the content experience. Moreover, as you design various areas of the content – for example, a product-detail web page – ensure that each area of the experience connects to this strategic vision.

This piece of work drives what types of content are necessary for an overall experience. You must understand the business objectives, content objectives, and needs of your content consumers. You must know for whom you are producing the content, what their needs are, and what the content must achieve. For specific documents – including web pages, areas within apps, user guides, product packaging, and sales materials – you will create a page-level content strategy (intent) later in the design phase. These page-level strategic intents will roll up to this overarching vision.

Understanding content lifecycle workflows

Content lifecycles are the powerhouse of your publishing model. Even the simplest forms of content publishing – creating a five-page website for a pizza parlor – possess a lifecycle. The content lifecycle represents the way each group within an organization works with content.

Figure 5.1 shows a high-level content lifecycle.

Figure 5.1 – Typical content lifecycle

Note that I have used a closed loop to indicate continual refinement and optimization of the content. I refer to this representation as high-level because each of these steps contains a series of substeps. As this model conveys, a person or group of people completes activities such as acquiring content from a source and creating or modifying it. Then, following review, the content is published, measured, and optimized.

An effective content lifecycle reflects the entire end-to-end process and accounts for each step and all associated substeps. As a starting point, most content lifecycles share similar high-level steps. But many become complicated. In international publishing models, localization is a key consideration, for instance. Depending on complexity, a lifecycle may contain several subprocesses or nuances within each process. Often a content lifecycle presents a framework of the end-to-end publishing processes for a content management system. When we implement a lifecycle or aspects of it into a content management system or other type of technology, we call these processes a workflow.

To create an effective model, you must identify all secondary and tertiary steps and vet each with the content team. With larger organizations and complicated lifecycles, you will want a business analyst to help capture and document the rules associated with each step in the lifecycle.

If your project contains a technology solution, ask for a technology architect to participate in this design process. The technology team must understand the implications of all workflow systems and assumptions, including offline or non-system workflow processes. The insight of the technology team can also help identify system constraints and determine which processes can be automated. The next two sections take you through the steps of lifecycle design.

Defining content types

Every content lifecycle starts with a *content type* because a content type determines the lifecycle necessary to support it. A video for new career seekers, for instance, possesses a different content lifecycle from a press release announcing a new job.

The very definition of a content type eludes many. Rebecca Schneider (Azzard Consulting) has noted to me that when she thinks of content types she likes to recall U.S. Supreme Court Justice Potter Stewart's words when he grappled with the definition of obscenity: "I know it when I see it." I agree with her, but I think we can frame the definition of a content type as a representation of the essence of the content itself. I am sure you understand clearly what I mean by that statement, so no further explanation is necessary. (I shall now duck from the bottles and foreign objects being hurled my way.)

I find that examples provide an excellent way to explain content types. Table 5.1 shows frequently used content types.

Table 5.1 – Common content types

Content type	Description
Annual reports	Financial or organization reports on the annual financials or health of a company or organization. Organizations are now creating interactive and multimedia reports. In this instance, content type is still "annual report," but the format is not a typical PDF or DOC format.
Biographies	Typically, corporate or organizational biographies of staff or leadership, but can include any type of biographical information about a person.
Calendar or event listings	Notable events for a business or organization. Can also be in the format of a calendar. In some cases, a company may include a calendar and an events list, which are distinct content types.
Contact information	Could include any array of information, including office location, email information, postal or mailing address, and phone/fax numbers.
Email	A category that could include various content types: announcements, newsletters, or recognition of a consumer such as an anniversary, birthday, confirmation of purchase, or user registration.
FAQ (frequently asked questions)	Questions and answers provided to consumers generally on products, services, and organization or use of a digital experience such as a website.
Forms	Any digital or print form that captures information. This category could include various content types: a registration form, a Contact Us web page, a user profile setup form, or a survey.
Images	Any type of image (JPG, PNG, GIF) used in digital or print publications.
Index, glossary, and table of contents	These content types could be part of a collection of content types included in front matter or end matter in publications. Each of these could constitute its own content type.
Infographics	Visual representations of data, generally in the form of images with text, such as a graph or chart.
Instructions	A category that could include various content types. For example, instructional text on a website for search or instructions on packaging such as cooking instructions.
Legal disclaimers	A category that could include various content types: copyright notice, liability statements, privacy policy, terms and conditions, and regulatory and compliance statements.
Maps	Visual or interactive maps, such as a map that indicates the location of a store.

Content type	Description
News	Announcements or noteworthy information about a person, company, or organization.
Blog posts	Blogs, generally reserved for influencers or notable people within a business or organization.
Podcasts, webinars	These two content types include audio (podcasts) or visual online presentations (webinars) or broadcasts.
Press releases	Organizational or business announcements to the press for a noteworthy story, event, or announcement.
Product details	Product details might surface on a product-detail page and include a product name, description, image, product key selling points, and benefits and specifications. Another content type may include product-category pages (a page representing a larger category, such as women's clothes).
Support or help content	A category that could include various content types: scripts for customer-support call centers, help pages in an application or digital experience, reference guides, or troubleshooting guides. FAQs could also be support content. Within your organization, this will need to be defined to avoid confusion.
User guides for product	A category that could include various content types: product quick-start guides, product manuals, or any type of instructions on how to use a product or service.
User-generated content	A category that could include various content types: comments, ratings and reviews, or content generated on social media sites such as Twitter, Facebook, and Instagram.
Tutorials	A category that could include various content types: online guides or videos, do-it-yourself content, or product user guides.
Videos	Recordings of moving images.
White papers	Documents that contain industry or thought leadership.

Often one content type contains several other content types embedded within it. For example, a press release that includes an infographic. Now some of you experts in content types are probably shaking your heads and rolling your eyes right now asking why I include email, videos and images. A format does not a content type make! True, although, technically speaking, videos and images per se are not specific formats unless I specify a GIF or MPEG.

Generally speaking, you should separate format types from content types. However, I include images and video – which could act as one of many content types if, for example, an annual report or tutorial is recorded in this media format – for one reason: videos and images often possess unique lifecycles that are critical to the content lifecycle definition process.

You will notice from Table 5.1 that many of these content types require different end-to-end processes to finalize content. For example, the content lifecycle for a tutorial video might include creating the content for the tutorial, shooting the video, editing the video, finalizing the video, and perhaps uploading it into a document-asset-management application, where metadata tagging occurs, before an editor links the video to a content management system.

That does not even include the vetting of actors or all of the substeps that go into video production. In contrast, a press release might possess a lifecycle more like this: a newsworthy event triggers a high-priority response; a writer captures the necessary components to piece together a story; an editor completes the first draft and submits it to a reviewer; the reviewer sends it back to the writer; the writer sends it to the legal department to be reviewed and finalized for embargo; and, finally, a marketing team disseminates it to press outlets via email and a website.

Complex? Yes. And, as you probably guessed, several substeps occur in this scenario as well.

At this point, you probably can see how content types play a significant role in an overall content ecosystem. Content types represent the main categories of content your organization produces and are critical inputs to other design deliverables, such as content lifecycles, *content models*, and taxonomies.

All content experiences start with a content type!

During the content-inventory process, you captured content types within the current ecosystem. You may have identified additional content types as part of the define phase. Defining a core set of content types helps you close out requirements for design, but you cannot finalize this list until the end of the design phase. You generally uncover additional content types as the design phase evolves.

Content type definition starts with the following steps:

1. Determine which content types your solution requires by reviewing the content types uncovered during the content-inventory.

2. Work with an information architect and the content team to uncover additional content types. You may want to conduct workshops or brainstorming sessions (including all stakeholders) to identify new content types for any future experience designs such as a new website or mobile app. Review the documentation from the assess phase for inspiration.

3. For externally consumed content experiences, review comparable materials, such as a competitor's website or sales materials.

4. Ensure that a copywriter has reviewed the content types. The same goes for a technology architect for technology solutions.

5. Capture the list of content types in a spreadsheet. Define each content type, and suggest an audience or targeted persona for each. This document will evolve into a content model later in the design phase.

6. You will probably continue defining content types throughout the design phase as additional types are uncovered. However, vet the initial list through all stakeholders and get their sign-off on the preliminary set.

Your content type definitions inform the overall content experience since they determine, at a high level, what constitutes the future-state content model. So make sure you confirm that the entire design team understands each content type and any implications or requirements from the types. Once you complete a list of known content types, you may begin defining the end-to-end content lifecycle for each.

Creating content lifecycle workflows

If content types made your head spin, then buckle up because the road down content lifecycle lane has even more twists, turns, and bumps. Sometimes when I do this work – and I do love doing it – I feel my brain needs a vacation. Content lifecycles can prove difficult, but once you complete this exercise, you will have designed a huge part of the content-publishing model.

The process of creating content lifecycles contains a series of steps for identifying, designing, and finalizing each necessary lifecycle. In terms of project timing, you can begin content lifecycle definition early within the design phase, but you should not expect final validation until the end of design phase. You should plan for the possibility of discovering new content types at any point during the design phase, which could force you to define another lifecycle. For example, a new website design might uncover additional content types late in the design phase. For projects with a technology component, you may discover additional technology requirements or constraints in the design phase that require you to redefine content lifecycles.

Since you probably documented current-state lifecycles in the assess and define phases, review the results of those phases to determine which lifecycles are missing. Then, survey your new content types and ask the content team to document lifecycles in the current state for each newly identified content type.

Do not worry if these lifecycles are not finalized or perfect. At this point you want to figure out which content types have similar or identical lifecycles. Capture any unique lifecycles. For each content type, ask yourself whether it shares the same lifecycle as other content types. This helps you identify how many lifecycles you must create. A workshop with the content team can prove useful in clustering content types with similar or shared lifecycles.

Next, capture the high-level steps within the organization's content lifecycles and supplementary processes, drawing from the content inventory, inputs in the planning phase, and stakeholder interviews. Call out all requirements (for example, "this content must be reviewed by legal and compliance"), exceptions, rules of use, gaps, and pain points in the current models. I often use whiteboards with sticky notes for this exercise.

Is your head spinning yet? Mine is. Let's break down these steps.

First, start with a workshop with the content team, and go through one content lifecycle at a time. Use a whiteboard or a pieces of poster-size paper taped across a wall. (Poster-sized sticky notes work perfectly for this exercise.) Create a table similar to Table 5.2. I generally plan for at least a half-day session and sometimes several full-day workshops, depending on the number of lifecycles required.

When conducting a workshop, I generally use sticky notes with each process or step, and I have the team plot each within the area where it should go. For example, the first step – Write content in a copy deck – could go in the Acquire column in the Copywriter row.

Table 5.2 – Content lifecycle exercise

	Acquire	Create	Review	Publish	Measure	Optimize
Chief editor						
Copywriter						
Brand reviewer						
Legal reviewer						
SEO reviewer						
Metadata tagging specialist						
Publisher						
Analytics team						
Editorial team						
Content strategist						
Content management system						
Document asset management system						

Start with the existing content lifecycles, and begin the session with each lifecycle plotted out from that exercise. As you go through each lifecycle, review the learnings from the assess and define phases, and ask the team to modify the existing lifecycles where pain points, gaps, or issues are present with either additional steps, the removal of unnecessary steps, or what the solution will require for new technology projects.

For example, if you are rolling out a new document asset management system, how should you modify the process to accommodate that new technology?

Ask the participants to plot out each process within the high-level lifecycle. See Table 5.3 for an example of what to capture for each area.

Table 5.3 – Content lifecycle steps and considerations

Lifecycle step	Considerations
Acquire	Document the entire content-acquisition process, including any assets, multimedia, or application files. Capture all content acquired, including content from third-party vendors, and list the processes involved. For example, how do third-party vendors supply multimedia files, and do the vendors retain the original source files?
Create	Document the content-creation process. Capture each method and content process. Example: first draft created by copywriter in a copy deck. Obviously, you can plot the action with the actor, in this case copywriter, and the state, first draft in copy deck.
Review	Note all the processes involved, both online and manual, including all roles and systems. Include review cycles and process flows for each decision process. Compare what happens when a reviewer either approves or rejects content. Capture all processes, including localization, translation, and syndication. If you include user-generated content, note the moderation processes.
Publish	Define the steps required to publish content, and note the release cycles and what happens to the content post-production. Capture how existing or published content gets updated and any specific workflow for high-priority publishing.
Measure	Note analytics processes, how efficacy of content is measured by a process or system, and how content is optimized. Include any SEO processes.
Optimize	Note any steps required to identify the way content will be optimized.
Archive (if necessary)	Note what happens to content when it is sunsetted (removed, deleted, or archived). If the organization never deletes or archives any content, then note this as a potential issue requiring further analysis. Also note when content should be expired. (expired content may not always be archived.) Capture any legal requirements for archival.

As you go through this process, include content from the following:

- Content migration or integration processes
- Syndication workflows
- User-generated content moderation or curated content
- Content messaging and/or re-messaging if it goes to more than one output (web, product packaging, customer call centers, etc.)
- Content regionalization, localization, and translation processes
- Digital-asset-management workflows
- Third-party vendors' content-creation processes

Verify that the workflow accounts for all necessary information. Show the business units, systems, documents, and processes that content flows through in its lifecycle. Include all distribution channels, platforms, and consumer-facing touchpoints. Note which formats the content takes as it goes from one step to the next. Examples:

- MS Word for acquisition via email
- MS Word for authoring in a copy deck
- Content entry into the content management system
- PDF format for review by brand and legal
- Comments function used in PDF by brand and legal
- Copy finalized in Microsoft Word
- Paste final copy into the content management system
- HTML output to website

Flesh out all subprocesses that roll up into the larger macro model, ensuring that each step links to another in the correct sequence from acquisition to publication.

Ok, are you ready for more page-turning suspense? You are almost there. To quote Jane Fonda's Workout Challenge, "We are in the homestretch; let's go for the burn."

Upon completing the workshop and capturing all of the lifecycles – current and future – you can create a swim-lane diagram in Microsoft Visio (PC) or OmniGraffle (Macintosh). (A swim-lane diagram demonstrates flows and processes; see Figure 5.2 for an example.) If you do not have access to either application, you can use presentation software such as Microsoft PowerPoint.

Work with a business analyst to complete this effort, as he or she will uncover additional requirements for detailed use cases. Confirm that the technology architect and business analyst understand all decisions made in this effort and that the business and technology requirements reflect the design decisions.

Notice how Figure 5.2 presents a high-level lifecycle and does not include all the substeps. Once you have the swim lanes documented, work with the business analyst, technology team, and content team to revise any areas of workflow where necessary. This effort might require multiple iterations between several teams. The content team should take the lifecycle back to each line of business and get validation.

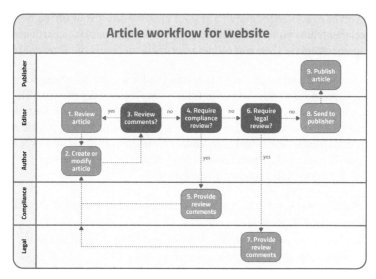

Figure 5.2 – Example content lifecycle in a swim-lane diagram

Often, these efforts have political implications within an organization. Be sensitive to teams that might be threatened by the automation of processes by making clear to each team the implications of improved systems. Often you can demonstrate that when a solution takes tedious work off people's plates, it frees them up to think more strategically about content or technology. Underscore the benefits of improved efficiency to allay the fears of job insecurity.

Finally, obtain sign-off from all necessary stakeholders on any workflow changes, and verify that efforts are in place to effectively manage any necessary changes.

And guess what? Voilà! You are finished. At least with lifecycle design.

Now let's turn to yet another complex effort: creating the page-level strategic intent.

Creating page-level strategic intent

Sometimes, people on user experience and digital design teams forget to consider the strategic intent of a page type and, thus, do not think through a framework or structure for which content should appear on each page type, template, or content type. I have witnessed this oversight even when a content strategist sat on the team!

If you have ever encountered a zealous creative director or interaction designer telling you which content is (or is not) necessary for a particular page or template, then you will appreciate the necessity of this exercise.

A page-level content strategy, sometimes called a strategic-intent document, provides a critical input to future-state content experiences. This document draws from the section titled "Creating a strategic intent for content experience" (p. 61) and positions content and content priorities for each page type, content type, and/or template within the new experience. If your work requires a consumer-facing content experience – digital or not – this exercise proves essential:

For each content type, page type, and template, this document should capture the following:

- What is the intent of the section or page? (that is, why does this page/content type/template exist?)
- What does the section or page need to achieve; what is the goal?
- What objectives do you need the content to achieve?
- Who is the audience?
- Which content is required to achieve those objectives and meet the audience needs? (Try to be more specific than just identifying content types. List specific content themes, such as: a rotating advertising image that changes seasonally.)
- What is the priority of the content? (For each type of content on the page, create a prioritization structure that can influence how often and where the content appears.)
- Which channels will the content reside on?

Obviously, draw from the business goals and objectives while completing this exercise. If every content experience – from a website home page to a news-and-events section – used such a tool prior to the design of the interaction, the web would be less cluttered with unusable and, frankly, horrible websites and pages.

Complete this exercise and get buy-in from the user experience team, the creative team, and any other stakeholders before starting design activities such as information architecture or visual design. Let me rephrase this important directive: make developing a page-level content strategy part of all design plans, and make successful completion of this step a prerequisite for wireframe and visual-design activities.

By defining a strategy for pages and content types, you can mitigate mistakes such as creating a NASCAR effect on a home page – tiles and tiles of disparate content like the ads on a race car. Maybe, just maybe, if we start enforcing this approach, we will see fewer websites – responsive websites often the worst offenders – that scroll indefinitely, one dissociated chunk of content after another.

This effort should serve not only interaction experiences but also every type of content you create, from product packaging to user guides.

Understanding the content brief, style guide, copy deck, model, and matrix

The activities detailed below can be completed in parallel with taxonomy and workflow design. These activities and deliverables frame the core design of a content approach. Each helps to inform the overall future-state content experience.

- **Content brief:** Similar to a creative brief, but with more detail on what the overall content approach should be. This document or series of documents defines the strategic direction of the content and answers such questions as what the content priorities are, for whom the content is written, and what the overall objective is. Development of this document should begin during the analysis of a project and continue into the design phase.
- **Content style guide (with voice and tone guidelines):** This document captures the editorial rules and standards for writing. It can be focused on the web or other media. Due to the amount of published information on style guides, this book does not offer additional insight on this matter. Wikipedia offers a list of commonly used guides (wikipedia.org/wiki/style_guide).
- **Content matrix:** A list of all content or content elements used on an external website. This document lists content modules, headers, subheaders, disclaimers, and any other types of content that are contained within a solution. The content matrix can evolve into a content model, a production matrix, or a market-rollout matrix that captures the location of translations and localized content.
- **Content model:** The design blueprint for the technology solution. This work embodies the culmination of a series of decisions and business requirements and captures the following elements in a digital experience: templates, the modules that make up each template, the elements and attributes of each module, the business logic and rules within the template, modules and elements, and all associated system data for the content.

■ **Copy deck:** A content entry tool for a copywriter, which captures all the consumer-facing copy. This document typically passes through brand and legal review. This document is usually authored in Microsoft Word and development is entirely manual. Often, a copy deck contains final copy that is then entered into either a content matrix or a content management system for publication. For consumer-facing websites, these documents do not generally show the copy within a larger context or user experience, so it can prove difficult for a brand or legal team to sign off until they have seen the copy in context.

■ **Additional content-creation tools:** There are many other tools used for content creation, including visual style guides for images and videos, briefs for campaigns that may also be used for video creation. Other tools include the messaging architecture, which takes the brand architecture and value proposition and creates an approach for content messaging. Margot Bloomstein covers this topic in her book, *Content Strategy at Work: Real-World Stories to Strengthen Every Interactive Project*[4].

Content matrix versus content model

Confusion may arise about the differences between a content model and a content matrix. A content matrix captures consumer-facing content. A content entry team (those who enter content into a content management system or consumer-facing content into an interactive application) uses a content matrix.

Think of a content matrix as a content-capture tool that shows the fields that are necessary for content creation. In many cases, the content matrix determines the fields that an author must use to enter content into a CMS for specific templates.

A technology development or implementation team uses the information in a content model to develop a tool, such as a content management system. A content model identifies system data and rules, and it offers content labels that must be hard-coded into system templates. It provides the content blueprint and architecture for static and dynamic content.

A content matrix and content model may be blended together since content matrixes often evolve into content models. A content model can also be used as a tool to map existing content to future-state experience for content migration efforts.

Creating a content matrix

The content matrix serves as a reference for the inventory, tracking, development, and maintenance of externally facing content through the life of the project. Model a content matrix from the templates and elements contained within a wireframe and site map (for example, Homepage → Hero Space → Header for Hero Space).

A content matrix should map to a wireframe and call out all necessary content elements within it. Therefore, this document represents the culmination of a series of decisions about which content goes into a page. A content strategist should work with the user experience team or information architect during the design process to close on content per wireframe and then use a matrix to capture those decisions. In this sense, a content matrix represents a process and requires several conversations and, often, design sessions with a user experience team to identify and close on necessary content per page type.

Table 5.4 – Sample content matrix structure

Sitemap ID #	WF ID	Page title	CMS template	Level 1 field	Level 2 field	Copy or label	URL
3.x.0	A	Madonna Rocks Home Page	Home Page	Hero Space	H1 title	Kevin P. Nichols' Product: "Madonna Rocks"	xpage.com/madonnarocks
3.x.0	A	Madonna Rocks Home Page	Home Page	Hero Space	H2 subtitle	Why she is still relevant	xpage.com/madonnarocks
3.x.0	A	Madonna Rocks Home Page	Home Page	Hero Space	Image alt text	Madonna in concert for MDNA Tour in 2013.	xpage.com/madonnarocks

You can see an example of a content matrix structure in Table 5.4. This example presents a framework for a typical content matrix. You may require additional fields depending on your content.

Table 5.5 shows the different pieces of information a content matrix might capture.

Table 5.5 – Types of fields a matrix could capture

Matrix field	Description
Sitemap ID#	Unique identifier for each page in the sitemap.
Wireframe ID#	ID number or title of the page as it resides in the sitemap.
Page title	A document title or HTML page title.
CMS template	The template to be used.
Level 1 field	Primary elements (level 1 fields) represent the first level of information within the page or template hierarchy. In some cases there will be a field to capture the information (such as a field found within a content management template). In other cases, there will be a copy deck. Also, a content matrix can be used as a content-capture tool where authors input the consumer-facing copy into it. Maps back to an area on the wireframe. You can develop as many levels as necessary to represent the content. (Example: *Madonna's Catalog | 2000s*.) A module, such as a product carousel, may require several levels of information, such as an image, header, subheader, and copy. For each, list in a separate field.
Level 2 field	Secondary elements (level 2 fields) are nested within a primary element and capture consumer-facing copy. (Example: *The Genius of Madonna in the 21st Century*.)
Level 3 field	Tertiary elements (level 3 fields) are nested within a secondary element and capture consumer-facing copy. (Example: *Madonna's Underappreciated and Grossly Misunderstood American Life Album*.) Note: You may have several levels further than level 3.
Copy or label	The text that goes into the field.
URL	The area within a digital experience where the page will reside. This information may not be necessary.

Other important considerations:

- For accessibility, account for alt text for images, and work this into your content-development process.
- Call out any page titles used in the browser bar of a webpage (HTML page titles). Example: *Madonna Just Might Be a Goddess home page*.
- Account for page-level metadata, such as page description and keywords.
- Have an SEO expert either provide you with or approve the metadata fields. In addition, HTML metadata descriptions, which search engines use to display a description under the page title, may require input or approval from editorial, brand, and legal reviewers.

A content matrix captures the final decisions regarding copy, or the fields required for copy, in a system. In other words, you may need copy decks or some other content-capture mechanism to work through the content reviews and finalize each area of content. Normally, I do not use content matrixes to complete content since many authors and reviewers find working within a content matrix cumbersome.

A well-designed content matrix builds in traceability between the content elements and the information architecture that defines the content's structure. Other documents, such as wireframes or graphic designs, might list and catalog content, but the content matrix provides the definitive source for content elements. A well-defined content matrix can evolve into a market matrix for translating and localizing content.

For dynamic content, a content matrix should provide only the structure. It cannot capture all content available within the dynamic content experience. As you develop the content matrix, emphasize to the project team that the structure for the matrix cannot be finalized until the user experience team finalizes wireframes. Furthermore, the content within the structure (the copy for each of the elements) cannot be finalized until the copy for each element is approved.

So if you are using the content matrix as a content entry tool, wait to populate content into it until the content team finalizes the matrix. Otherwise, significant rework may be required.

To complete a content matrix, follow these steps:

1. Ensure that you are a part of all content-related discussions and design sessions with the information architect, business analyst, and any other user experience team members. Conduct a series of sessions with the user experience team to determine which content should surface on each page type, template, or page. Use a page-level strategic intent document to frame the discussions (see the section titled "Creating page-level strategic intent" (p. 73)).
2. Survey all requirements, including the content style guide, site map, wireframes, content inventory, content audit, and any relevant current-state findings.
3. Create a list of all known content for the site using the content matrix template. For examples, see my website.[2]
4. Use the elements described below as a starting point, and flesh out relevant details. The content team, the information architect, and any other content stakeholders should validate this work.

---

[2] http://kevinpnichols.com/cs/

Similar to the taxonomy, the content matrix is a living document. Anytime an organization adds a new type of content or template to a content experience – or changes one – the content matrix must be updated.

Creating a content model

Creating a content model amounts to a significant effort for an enterprise content strategist and the content team. I have seen content models that amount to a hundred or more pages when printed. The technology team uses a content model to understand the following:

- Content types required for a digital experience
- System templates that map to the content types
- Fields and modules within a template (often referred to as *objects* for content management systems)
- Rules regarding the use of content and the way each field or module should perform
- Metadata and other tags necessary at the template, page, and module level
- Structural considerations such as what content resides in which templates and in what order

Projects that need significant rules or logic built into the content – for example to handle personalization, cross-sell, or up-sell – require a content model. This model should capture the sitemap ID, wireframe ID, page name, and module name. Under the module name, the following might be captured:

- **Character count:** Maximum, minimum of characters for the module.
- **Channel population:** Channel consideration that indicates on which channels content should be published, for example: mobile tablet, mobile smartphone, mobile feature phone, and desktop website.
- **Content rules:** Any logic or necessary rule that requires technology integration. Examples: "this content maps to x user for personalization" or "if a user searches on x and arrives at the site, serve up x type of content."
- **Targeted users:** Any personas or segments.

The list above is not exhaustive; you must work with the technology team at the beginning of the project to determine which rules and considerations your content model should capture. Table 5.6 provides a sample list of content model fields with descriptions.

Table 5.6 – Content model fields

Content model Field	Description
ID #	Identifies each piece of content uniquely.
ID # of wire-frame, sitemap, etc.	Identifies number or title of the page as it resides within the sitemap or wireframe. You can also call out the functional specification to which the content maps. Use this to build in traceability from the content model and wireframe, sitemap, or functional specifications. Use the same numbering system throughout.
CMS template	Names the CMS template used in the content management system.
Content type	Identifies the type of content. Examples: press release, product-detail page, etc.
Content object or module (level 1–x)	Names the content object or module. Make sure you create fields for each level of information.
Persona or consumer target	Identifies whom the content is targeted for when personalizing an experience.
Authenticated	Designates whether authentication is necessary or not (usually just yes or no). Authenticated content requires a person to log into an application or user profile.
Format	Identifies the format, such as: PDF, JPG, MPEG, etc.
Max./min. character length	Indicates the maximum/minimum number of characters.
New/migrated	Indicates the content is either new or pulled from an existing system. Use this field for projects requiring content migration.
Source	Indicates if the content is pulled from another system, such as a product catalog database or syndicated feed.
Other rules	Required when any other business rules or logic is necessary for which the other fields fail to account. E.g., additional personalization rules.
Metadata	Required for any metadata for the system, page, object, or module.

The following steps can help you design a content model:

1. Work with a member of the technology team at the beginning of the design phase to determine which fields you need to capture in the content model. Also consult the business analyst.

2. Define your content types. You may add content types during the design process.

3. As the user experience team finalizes each wireframe and the content matrix is closed, use the content model to capture the content types, the templates that map to each, and the modules within each template. A template does not map one-to-one with a page or even a content type. A template provides the structure and format to house content, such as a home-page template, a product-detail template, an article template, and so forth. Often, one template can be applied to many types of pages within the experience.

4. For each module, capture the rules, logic, and other necessary information related to content requirements.

5. Work with a business analyst to define the business rules and logic related to each content element. The business analyst should capture the business requirements in a functional specification; the content model should capture content-specific rules. The content strategist's work does not replace a business-requirements matrix, detailed use cases, or functional specifications, all of which are necessary for technology implementation efforts.

Authoring the editorial guidelines

Editorial guidelines are different from a content style guide. They provide authoring guidelines for creating content for a specific experience, for example, website editorial guidelines. A content style guide informs voice and tone, and it creates rules related to style, grammar, terminology, etc. In contrast, editorial guidelines may reference voice and tone from the content style guide, but the focus is on how to create content for a home page, a product-landing page, a user guide, etc.

Do you remember the task of creating a page-level strategic intent? In the editorial guidelines, you document that strategy and provide instructions for tasks such as writing copy or selecting what type of content to include for a particular document type or page. Well-written editorial guidelines include sample copy along with recommendations for dealing with video and multimedia.

To complete this effort, create an outline similar to the following:

- Strategic intent of the experience
- Voice and tone considerations (from the content style guide)
- Page-level objectives (primary and secondary)
- Recommended content for each page or document type
- Sample text and screen shots of similar pages that incorporate a best-in-class editorial experience

Flesh out the document and ask an information architect and copywriter review it. You will probably vet this document through an editorial review board, governance structure, or marketing and branding team. Write this guide from the viewpoint of authoring and editing content and creating pages (such as bringing content together in a CMS). Also make sure this guide exists before any major authoring or content creation occurs for a new experience.

Building logic into content experience

When you build intelligence into content solutions, you create an experience where content surfaces to a consumer based upon certain rules or logic. Such experiences apply to both internal systems and consumer-facing systems. There are different types of content intelligence, but for the scope of this guide, these are primary:

- **Cross-sell/up-sell:** Used in e-commerce to recommend one product when a consumer selects or views another. For example, Victoria wants to buy a new dress on a tablet website. Once she finds the perfect skirt, she notices recommendations for a matching belt, shoes, and necklace. This experience is driven by taxonomy, business rules, and associated metadata.
- **Recommendation logic:** Used in any type of digital experience where one piece of content accompanies related or recommended content. Example: "Customers who purchased this recording also bought that." Recommendation logic is driven by taxonomy and decision trees with business rules and associated metadata. (A recommendation engine can suggest a product on a consumer-facing website based on the purchases of other users.)
- **Personalization:** Any type of contextually relevant content directed to a consumer. Driven by persona or segmentation models as manifested in taxonomical nodes, business rules, and associated metadata. You can personalize content to a consumer based on any of the following:
  - ☐ Who the consumer is
  - ☐ Where the consumer is

☐ Which device the consumer is using

☐ What the consumer is trying to achieve (for example, buy a specific product)

☐ How the consumer interacts with the content (for example, the browse path, click-stream, or point of entry such as landing on a website from a keyword search term)

☐ When the consumer is engaged with the digital experience

■ **Semantic web:** Specifies the relationships between units of content. Includes predictive search. (Predictive search populates content into a search field based on previous searches before the user completes an entire term or phrase.) Driven by ontology and associated metadata.

Personalization becomes even more complicated because it can track authenticated (logged-in) and unauthenticated states. A consumer logged into an application generally has a profile and has completed certain activities that can be tracked. Therefore, content can be served up to an authenticated user in a relevant and timely manner because the system possesses certain information about him or her, such as gender, birthday, location, purchase history, and preferences.

An unauthenticated user can still be tracked on a website via point of entry. Entry points may include a search that leads the consumer to the site, a banner that a consumer clicks on, a link from another website, or a consumer typing the home-page URL. Additionally, behavior can be tracked while the consumer is on the website (where he or she came from, the clickstream on the site, the duration per page, etc.).

You can also track how many other visits to the site the consumer has completed. And content can be triggered based on a content consumer's action while perusing the website. Finally, a digital experience can serve up content to a consumer based on his or her location, time of day, and local events.

If your final experience requires personalization, you should have a persona or segmentation node within a taxonomy. Any type of person-alization will require a map that shows how each targeted persona or customer maps to a specific piece of content. This effort will require validation on behalf of the business analyst. You should work with the entire design team to capture all necessary data required within a consumer profile. For large companies, this will require analysis of and integration with data about customers and their behaviors captured by a customer relationship management tool.

You will have to carry out a mapping exercise that lists user types or consumer actions, maps each to specific types of content, and defines the rules for when and to whom content displays. For a guide to best practices in content strategy and personalization, see my presentation, *Content Strategy for the Customer Journey: Personalization Done Right.*[3]

Best practices for personalization:

- Define the personalization goals and a roadmap. Create a visual of what personalization looks like at launch, nine months post-launch, and fifteen months later. (You can use any sequencing, such as launch, six months later, etc.) A personalization strategy evolves over time. At launch, you may not be able to have an enhanced personalization experience. But you can identify what you think the customer journey will be on your site and serve relevant content. Moreover, you can figure out which information to track so the technology team launches the site properly.

- Work with an information architect or user researcher to identify the correct users, personas, and consumer targets and to map each to the appropriate content.

- Involve a member of the technology team who should also validate all the user types and entitlements.

- Ensure that this technology team member remains present in all discussions and decisions to guarantee that technology is created to support each instance of personalization.

- Capture and document all metadata information that comes out of the personalization effort.

For details related to these types of content experiences and ways to design for each, see Ann Rockley's *Managing Enterprise Content*[17].

Designing for omnichannel and multichannel experiences

You can no longer afford to design for a single-channel experience unless you are creating content for a platform like Xbox 360 or a standalone app. Ann Rockley speaks at length about how to set up adaptive and structured content in a manner that facilitates multichannel proliferation. I will not provide detail on that here since Ann covers it in *Managing Enterprise Content*. I will provide a few principles for consideration, however, including some best practices for omnichannel experiences.

---

[3] http://www.slideshare.net/kpnichols/content-strategy-personalizationcustomerjourney-confab2013

Let's start with responsive versus adaptive approaches. Responsive design works best when channels share the same content. If you have the *same content* for desktop websites, tablet, and mobile smartphone websites, responsive design works well. Responsive design does not function as a content solution, but rather exists as a design solution for optimizing a design across different channels.

If you have unique or channel-optimized content – and I am going to go out on a limb here and say that in most cases users expect to accomplish different tasks in each channel – then a responsive-only approach is insufficient. You will need an adaptive approach, which allows for unique content in each channel.

Use a responsive approach for content shared across devices; use an adaptive approach for content that changes across devices. You may leverage a hybrid approach of the two within the same digital experience.

When considering multichannel, there are three types of content. By identifying which content falls into these categories, you can frame an approach (adaptive, responsive, hybrid) that works best for your content needs:

- **Shared content:** This type of content remains the same regardless of channel. For example, a company logo.
- **Shared-but-edited content:** This type of content remains the same thematically but is edited to optimize it for different channels. For example, a long product description for a desktop website, a medium-sized one for a product package, and a short one for a mobile smartphone website. A smart approach structures templates so that shared-but-edited content can be captured in one place.
- **Unique per channel:** This type of content exists in only one or two channels or is specific per channel. A QR scan function on a mobile smartphone exemplifies this concept because you would most likely not include this feature on a desktop website.

These three concepts are critical to best practices in developing content for an omnichannel experience. Remember when we discussed omnichannel in Chapter 1? The diagram in Figure 5.3 shows how to convey the way a customer engages with content within the omni experience.

Figure 5.3 – A customer-engagement model for omnichannel

From Figure 5.3, you can see that a content consumer engages in channels differently and, thus, expects each channel to meet specific needs. To support omnichannel experiences, you need a scalable, structured, and modular approach to content management and publishing. Ann Rockley writes extensively on what she terms *intelligent content*, content that's structured in a way that makes it adaptive and scalable within an enterprise. Her approach also sets up content successfully for omnichannel.

To summarize key themes for best practices, Ann presents a framework for successful content:

- **Structured:** Content that lives within a structure. A system that structures content, labels it, and sets it up for reuse, independent of presentation. Structured content can be reused in more than one channel or experience. For omnichannel, a taxonomy offers one way to structure content and is critical when you have many channels because the output channel becomes a facet within the taxonomy.
- **Modular:** Modules reside in a structure and often appear in templates. Modular content (a product description, a carousel on a homepage, etc.) is created once and reused in multiple places. If you update a

module, you update all the places where it appears. You can tag modules with metadata to enable delivery of content based on context, such as user, persona, device, or location. Together, modular and structured content allow you to embrace the power of content management by establishing reusable, findable, nimble, and agile content.

- **Reusable:** A characteristic which means you can reuse a module or piece of content in more than one experience and channel. Thus, you could publish the same content to a product package as well as a desktop website.
- **Metadata:** Metadata enables intelligent content. Metadata provides information that systems can use to determine where and how content appears and to facilitate search by consumers. Metadata enables advanced features, such as personalization, that are essential for omnichannel experiences.
- **Format free:** An independent presentation layer controls how content renders. Thus, content can appear in multiple channels and platforms without causing presentation issues.

Following the direction that Ann Rockley puts forth will help you create flexible and adaptable content for multiple channels and experiences.

A few other key considerations for omnichannel content:

- Omnichannel content is user-centered and consumer-focused, so to develop it correctly, look at the business goals and objectives and the consumer needs and tasks, and identify which cross-channel journeys the content consumer engages to accomplish a task. For example, what does he or she do to purchase a product? From which channels does she or he jump to complete one task after another?
- Identify your user journeys, then work backwards from the channels they engage and what they do in those channels to define your content experience for each. You should also think of structuring your content-publishing processes using this approach (user and content type) instead of around internal lines of business.
- Create a roadmap that defines at least an eighteen-month plan. You can see an example of a roadmap in Chapter 4. Omnichannel is a huge undertaking that links all channels. The most difficult aspects are creating the internal integration to support it and figuring out how to capture the correct metrics throughout the cross-channel experience to sustain it (for example, how to track what a consumer does when he or she jumps from one channel to the next).

My slideshare at http://slideshare.net/kpnichols contains several presentations on how to do omnichannel content strategy effectively. I plan to continue to evolve the theme of omnichannel content strategy.

Creating a taxonomy and metadata

Taxonomy and metadata are complicated topics. This book does not attempt to function as a definitive source on taxonomy or metadata creation. There are books out there to show you exactly how to undergo this effort (see the section titled "Additional reading" at the end of this chapter for some examples).

You will want a skilled taxonomist and metadata specialist on the project to assist you with this endeavor. This topic and this section are fairly dense. In fact, if a taxonomy does not directly affect you or if people on your team have this topic covered, you may choose to move on to the next chapter.

The Glossary contains definitions of many of the terms used here and elsewhere in the book. Terms that are defined in the glossary are highlighted in *italics*.

Creating metadata

You will use *metadata* in nearly all types of enterprise content strategy engagements. Effective metadata creation requires the expertise of a metadata specialist or a content strategist with this type of experience. Additional logic and inheritance, as well as a definition of the standards and authoring practices, are required for a seamless strategy. A *controlled vocabulary* (*taxonomy*) is a starting point for this, but additional work is required.

This section illustrates the high-level steps required to create metadata:

1. Review all metadata schemas within the organization. Analyze any XML schemas and data models. Compare this work against your requirements and the findings from the current-state assessment.
2. Select a metadata standard with the content team and technology architect. Consider the Dublin Core (dublincore.org) standard, a well-regarded standard for metadata. Note that many standards are industry specific.
3. Determine which tags are system-generated and which are user-generated.
4. Determine which metadata every template will use based on content types and any rules for intelligent content, such as personalization. Also define and review any system-generated metadata.

5. Account for all inheritance schemes and models. Define parent-to-child relationships and any other associated relationships. You can use a spreadsheet to detail when and where to place elements.
6. For websites and portals, incorporate SEO requirements and vet decisions with an SEO expert.
7. After you have compiled a robust list of metadata elements, create a metadata guidebook. This document should include training materials for first-time users, rules for using metadata, and an authoring how-to guide.

Now that we understand the key steps in metadata creation, we can turn to examining how technology can support a robust metadata engine.

Metadata and taxonomy technology solutions

You can use a technology solution, such as a metadata-tagging or a taxonomy-management application, to manage and tag information. Technologies also exist to manage *ontologies* and *thesauri*. A content management system often bundles taxonomy and metadata-management functionality as part of the application.

Work with a technology architect to determine which technologies best meet your project requirements. These tools are not an end in themselves. A taxonomy specialist needs to define and optimize terminology and ensure that it meets evolving business needs. Similar to content audits, no technology exists for content organization or structure that does not require the expertise of a person.

While you should consult with a technology architect to evaluate vendors, your business requirements and content requirements, many of which are uncovered in the current-state assessment phase, should drive the selection of a technology solution. It is a bad idea to make a technology decision without content or business requirements. You'll end up trying to retrofit your requirements to the solution.

Developing a taxonomy

Taxonomies are integral to enterprise content strategy since these tools structure content, label information, facilitate search, and assist with system integration. However, taxonomies are costly to develop and maintain. The enterprise content strategist and the content team should recognize that a taxonomy project doesn't have a beginning and an end. A taxonomy requires ongoing effort and maintenance.

Maintaining a taxonomy requires a scalable and extensible infrastructure. Make sure that stakeholders understand the evolving nature of a taxonomy. When the content team signs off on a taxonomy, it agrees on the structure, labels, and terms of a current snapshot, not a final, unchanging deliverable.

Canned taxonomies exist, but they can present challenges and limits; I don't recommend using a canned taxonomy for an enterprise content strategy. Like content management systems, off-the-shelf taxonomies require customization and ongoing support for effective results.

Stakeholders are accountable not only for maintaining a taxonomy but also for continued development, which will be necessary as business objectives evolve.

Other considerations:

- An enterprise taxonomy often comprises several taxonomies.
- A taxonomy is system-independent and often system-agnostic. Content consumer and business requirements drive what goes into a taxonomy.
- Taxonomies must evolve and progress as the business changes.
- Taxonomies require governance for maintenance and evolution.

The following suggestions do not provide a comprehensive guide to taxonomy development. Rather, they contain best practices and key steps within the process. If you do not have taxonomy expertise, then consider employing a taxonomy professional to complete this work.

Before building the taxonomy, consider the following preparatory tasks:

- Identify the relevant stakeholders. This includes people who must weigh in, review, and approve the effort. Conduct interviews so that you understand the business context and taxonomy use cases.
- Create a list of terms that are used within the organization. These include all content types, consumer-facing search terms, and any categorization schemes based on the content inventory. In addition, take into consideration anything that relates to the future-state content scope. Ask for any existing taxonomies, metadata schemas, data models, glossaries, or lists of acronyms. Product catalogs are often derived from a taxonomy.
- From the content inventory, survey the content types and determine how to identify each with appropriate labels.
- Capture any synonyms or additional terms a content consumer might use to search for the information.

■ Capture any related terms associated with each preferred (or primary) term.

■ If you require a *faceted taxonomy*, make sure that the content team has adequate time to validate each facet.

Now you are ready to decide on the taxonomy model (or models; more than one taxonomy may be necessary for an enterprise content strategy). From all of the information gleaned during the current-state analysis, the content team should determine if a *faceted taxonomy* is required. You will need a faceted taxonomy for projects requiring *parametric navigation*. Note that a taxonomy is not the same as navigation; a taxonomy organizes information and content based on the essence of that content.

The following steps present a blueprint for best practices. Consider each for a taxonomy engagement.

1. Build the taxonomy, revisiting the current-state analysis and completing the following steps in concert with the content team. Be sure to include a business analyst and, especially, a technology architect. Do not build an enterprise taxonomy without continual validation from a technology architect.

2. Extract categories, subcategories, and tertiary categories (use as many levels as necessary) from each document in the content inventory that has been identified as necessary for the future-state design. While doing so, decide on labels to identify each category. The results of this exercise must be approved by the content team.

3. Sort the categories, and create new categories related to topics or the essence of the content that each category captures. Agree on nomenclature for each, capturing synonyms as you complete this process. Also capture any abbreviations or alternate terms. Consider the capabilities of the search engine while you do so. Search-engine rules often include variants and misspellings as part of general business rules. This keeps the taxonomy from becoming too cumbersome and difficult to manage.

4. Address all gaps, missing content, and issues identified in the current-state analysis. The taxonomy should only account for content that will be available at launch. Otherwise, you are creating terms for content that will not exist, which can frustrate content consumers. As a living document, a taxonomy expands over time to accommodate new content types in the future. Once content is available, a taxonomy can be updated to account for it. A "build it and they will come" strategy seldom proves effective.

5. Validate every category by reviewing which elements are required at the lowest levels of the hierarchy. Manage only metadata or taxonomies that you are using. This bottom-up validation ensures that the taxonomy reflects the present business requirements. Answer the following:

   ■ How many pieces of content belong to a category?
   ■ Where does the content come from?
   ■ How do the categories relate to one another?

6. If your content team decides it's necessary to leverage equivalent terms for particular terms, then create a *synonym ring* that captures equivalent terms used by different groups. For example, you might have one group that uses the term *money* and another that uses the term *currency*. Do the same with each piece of content that belongs to each category grouping. Account for competitive terms. However, **do not** use competitors' branded names or labels to drive traffic to your site. This approach can create a legal liability.

7. Conduct a preliminary review with the technical architect, legal team, brand team, and any other internal organizations responsible for compliance. As stated previously – and the emphasis is intended – include a member of the technology team throughout this process to account for technology constraints.

8. Validate that you account for all content by reviewing the content inventory and materials that were generated during the current-state analysis in the assess phase.

9. Conduct card-sorting exercises[5] with the content team, and test the results with content consumers to support user-centered design and relevant nomenclature. The content team can prepare for this exercise by completing virtual card-sorting activities on their own. They can then offer their insights to the larger group. During the card-sorting exercise, note any gaps (missing terms) or issues (missing content) that require solutions.

10. Validate user-centered design, usability, and relevant nomenclature through consumer-facing (and in this case, end-user) testing. This is an essential step because taxonomies are consumer-facing solutions that inform website structure, parametric navigation, filtered search, etc.

11. Flesh out as many levels as necessary within the overall taxonomy. If your project requires personalization, then factor in facets for personas, segments, customer journeys, or profile-driven require-

---

[5] Wikipedia has a useful article on card sorting that also has references to additional information: http://wikipedia.org/wiki/Card_sorting.

ments. Later, you will need to develop a matrix to show which pieces of content map to which user profiles.

12. Define the terms used in the taxonomy.

Whew. All that for just a little taxonomy. Now are you ready for happy hour? Or maybe a good run in the woods to clear your mind? We are nearly there in terms of taxonomy, but a few more steps are still required. Let's talk about creating metadata to support the taxonomy.

1. After completing the initial taxonomy – all levels are fleshed out and all categories, subcategories, and variables are known – assign metadata as necessary. Elements within the taxonomy (for example, category, subcategory, level 3 category, etc.) can also be metadata.

2. Create metadata for terms in the taxonomy. You can use a synonym ring or thesaurus to do this. For example, the term *cat* has synonyms, such as *feline*, *kitty*, and *kitten*. You may not need to define metadata for every term in your taxonomy; some elements can inherit metadata from the category where they reside. Also, subcategories can inherit information from the primary category. For example, if the categories are Feline → Cat → Persian, and the term *cat* has the metadata noted above, then *Persian* can inherit all the terms associated with *cat*.

3. Create consumer-facing nomenclature when relevant. Include a field that captures this information in the taxonomy. Assign all relevant elements consumer-friendly labels. For consumer-facing websites, test the nomenclature through a series of usability tests with content consumers.

4. Define the metadata rules of use. Create an additional column in your spreadsheet titled "Metadata Rules of Use," and note any required logic, for example, "Inherit all metadata from level 2 with level 3 elements." If appropriate, implement a thesaurus that links similar terms together. This will inform the search engine and assist content consumers in finding the necessary information. These rules may be used by technology systems, content managers, or both.

The above steps should result in a spreadsheet that looks similar to Table 5.7.

Table 5.7 – Sample taxonomy structure

Level 1	Level 2	Level 3	Synonyms	Consumer-facing nomenclature	System metadata rules
Legal					
	War-ranty		Certificate of guarantee, guar-antee, warranty promise, limited warranty	Warranty	
		Com-plete war-ranty state-ment		Complete warranty statement	Inherit all metadata values and level 2 synonyms

We have now completed the taxonomy exercise. You can probably see why librarians – with their keen organization skills, attention to detail, and love for information management – make the best taxonomists. Of course, the fact that most of them study taxonomies and metadata and are experts on this science adds to their appeal. I welcome those with library-science backgrounds to participate in efforts requiring taxonomy work. Librarians also often make excellent content strategists.

At this point, you can take a deep breath and let out a long exhale. We are almost ready to put the taxonomy considerations to rest (for now, at least), but consider this final thought: get buy-in from a business or organization to invest in a taxonomy in the first place.

Selling an enterprise taxonomy

Enterprise taxonomies bring immense value to an organization when they are designed, implemented, and maintained correctly. But an enterprise taxonomy can be costly. It requires continual attention, and you need resources to build, grow, and maintain it. Thus, you might have to sell it to a management team within an organization. To do so, emphasize the benefits of an enterprise taxonomy:

- Disambiguates terms and reduces search errors
- Enables cross-sell and up-sell in consumer-facing interfaces
- Enables multisourced content
- Enables systems to be integrated across an enterprise with a controlled and structured vocabulary

- Improves user experience through consistency across brand channels
- Enforces publishing standards by overseeing the consistent use of terms within the content domain
- Facilitates content reuse
- Facilitates personalization by creating a set of terms that map to defined target consumers, which then serve content according to each user type, persona, or segment
- Gets the highest quality and most relevant content to the right user at the right time in the most efficient manner possible
- Helps the content consumer retrieve information with appropriate and consistent content labels
- Provides an organization structure that enables easy navigation or *parametric search*, which speeds searching
- Supplies the terms necessary for recommendation engines

All of these benefits can translate to enormous business value, and you should highlight them to ensure that the primary stakeholders understand why a taxonomy can prove invaluable to an organization's success.

Additional reading

The following sources are essential reading for anyone involved in the development of taxonomies:

- Aitchison, Jean, Alan Gilchrist, and David Bawden. *Thesaurus Construction and Use: A Practical Manual*[2].
- Hedden, Heather. *The Accidental Taxonomist*[9].
- Stewart, Darin L. *Building Enterprise Taxonomies*[19].

For an excellent presentation on the importance of metadata and nimble content, see Rachel Lovinger's presentation "Make Your Content Nimble"[13].

See also Rachel Lovinger's Nimble content report "Nimble: a razorfish report on publishing in the digital age"[14].

For additional information on how to design content solutions, particularly intelligent content design, see Ann Rockley and Charles Cooper's *Managing Enterprise Content: A Unified Content Strategy*[17].

Another excellent resource for content design is Margot Bloomstein's *Content Strategy At Work*[4].

CHAPTER 6
Build Phase

GOVERN

3. Build

During the build phase, you work with a technology team to ensure that your design work – taxonomy, content model, lifecycles, etc. – is properly implemented. This phase is often referred to as development or implementation.

As a part of this phase, you may complete some or all of these activities:

■ planning for new content creation
■ creating a content migration approach and plan
■ designing or creating a content calendar

Depending on the project, you may want to keep an enterprise content strategist on the team to oversee how the technology team implements the content design requirements. When the technology is tested, you will want to make sure it functions as expected.

You may ask, why include content planning and content calendar creation in the build phase? These steps cannot occur until certain aspects of design are finalized. However, in projects with multiple phases of design or agile projects, these activities can occur before the end of the design phase. If your project has an agile or batch approach to design, you can begin content planning for each sign-off batch, for example: batch 1: home page complete; batch 2: product pages complete; etc.

A batch constitutes a group of functions, pages, or templates that some project approaches use to accelerate the design process. In agile projects, these are known as stories. I recommend completing at least two batches in the design phase and having at least two levels of the sitemap approved for interactive experiences before starting any content planning or creation. Otherwise, you run the risk of the designs changing. I recommend erring on the side of caution before beginning these activities. If you begin content creation too early and the design changes, you will create additional work, which can translate into large cost overruns. It can be worse if you start content migration for a large-scale project too soon.

A copywriter may be able to help flesh out some labels and nomenclature during the design process. But do not create significant new content – copy, images, videos, etc. – until you have completed the design phase or at least several stories or batches. If you receive push-back on this approach from other stakeholders, make sure that all stakeholders understand the risks involved, including the possibility of time, effort, and money wasted developing incorrect or unnecessary content.

This chapter will show you how to create a content plan, account for content migration, and create a content calendar.

Creating the content plan

Content in this context means all content for the new experience. Planning refers to all activities required to get final content into the system. Work with a project manager when creating a content plan.

To create a content plan, use the content called out in the content matrix as a starting point. This plan should account for the acquisition, creation, review, and publication of content. Assign someone to track content status as part of the process. Consider translation and localization processes, if necessary. Also account for the tasks necessary for image, video, Flash/Java, and multimedia content.

Let's look at it step-by-step:

1. After you complete the content matrix, sort it by content type. Create a separate worksheet or plan for each type of content. For example, an image requires different steps than a product-details page.
2. Include all the relevant information in the plan for each content type. Information to consider: content type name, placement or rules, metadata, and source.
3. Identify the volume and scope of content for each content type (how many pages, images, modules, etc.)
4. Refer to the content lifecycles to figure out each step necessary for content creation. List the steps out and work with a project manager to build a plan based on the processes. Example:
   - **Task 1:** acquire content requirements
   - **Task 2:** create first initial copy
   - **Task 3:** submit copy for initial review, etc.
5. Assign a level of effort for each step, factoring in complexity. For example, you could use three levels: low for low-complexity content, medium for medium complexity, high for high complexity.
6. Assign time to each step based on the metric (high, medium, low).
7. Estimate the volume of high-, medium-, and low-complexity content, then estimate the amount of time required to develop each type of content. (A project manager will know how to complete this effort.)

8. Create due dates for each step in the process. Identify owners for either the content itself or for each step in the process.

9. Work with the PM to figure out how many resources are needed to complete the effort.

10. Ensure that the PM understands how to manage and track the effort.

Figure 6.1 shows a sample content creation plan for images. Notice how the image name and areas with which it resides (in this case, the hero space on a home page of a website) is identified.

Name	Owner	Identify Image	Create Image	Brand Review	Revise Image	Legal Review	Finalize	Approve	Asset Handoff	DAM Entry
Thumbnail	Helga	12-Jul	13-Jul	14-Jul	14-Jul	16-Jul	20-Jul	20-Jul	20-Jul	21-Jul
Thumbnail	Samir	12-Jul	13-Jul	14-Jul	14-Jul	16-Jul	20-Jul	20-Jul	20-Jul	21-Jul
Thumbnail	Helga	12-Jul	13-Jul	14-Jul	14-Jul	16-Jul	20-Jul	20-Jul	20-Jul	21-Jul
Thumbnail	Samir	12-Jul	13-Jul	14-Jul	14-Jul	16-Jul	20-Jul	20-Jul	20-Jul	21-Jul
Hero 1	Helga	12-Jul	13-Jul	14-Jul	14-Jul	16-Jul	20-Jul	20-Jul	20-Jul	21-Jul
Hero 2	Samir	12-Jul	13-Jul	14-Jul	14-Jul	16-Jul	20-Jul	20-Jul	20-Jul	21-Jul
Hero 3	Helga	12-Jul	13-Jul	14-Jul	14-Jul	16-Jul	20-Jul	20-Jul	20-Jul	21-Jul
Hero 4	Samir	12-Jul	13-Jul	14-Jul	14-Jul	16-Jul	20-Jul	20-Jul	20-Jul	21-Jul

Figure 6.1 – Sample content-creation plan for image creation

If the matrix contains too much detail, then you can use a page-level plan, which means you look at steps required to create a page, such as a home page. However, many experiences reuse modules, such as video modules, in which case planning should be at that level. A separate plan can account for the completion of each task.

Do all of these considerations sound complex? Content planning is no simple task. That's why I recommend collaborating with a seasoned project manager who has experience with content plans. You can use a tool like Microsoft Project, but I think a spreadsheet works better for content planning. A project manager or traffic manager should manage this process and the production plan.

Additional considerations:

■ Legal, brand, and compliance reviewers may have to fit content reviews into their already busy schedules. Ensure that you understand their time limitations and work that into the plan. A project manager will understand how to factor duration into the schedule.

■ Set expectations, and keep stakeholders informed as content gets completed. Completion and rollout of a content management system or website does not equate to completion of the content that must go into it. Early in the project-plan process, leave a placeholder for content creation, migration, and production.

■ Be realistic about content creation. Do not try to sandwich it in during the implementation phase of a content management system, just so it is complete at the end of the content management system rollout. Often content creation requires much time and several iterations. If you are expected to have content complete by the end of implementation, then you may have to prioritize what is absolutely essential for product or digital experience launch and set the expectation that future releases will build on the content experience.

You should also have the project manager create a weekly or even daily status sheet. You will want to report back to the content stakeholder team weekly or daily, depending on the need. Since content production can push back deadlines for product launches, digital experience launches, etc., a transparent reporting process can help set expectations with stakeholders. A status sheet generally contains information at the page level and tracks completion of each page. Work with a project manager to ensure this level of tracking happens.

Accounting for content migration

When is content migration required? When you are developing a new system or experience and wish to retain a portion of existing content. Although you should identify any need for content migration during the assess and define phases, you will complete most migration activities during the build phase.

Migration activity across phases

Because migration should be understood in its entirety, I have grouped all the migration activities together in this chapter rather than address each in different sections of the book. I have noted here which activities occur in which phases.

Plan phase: Determine whether you will need to migrate content. If you think the future-state content experience will require existing content, which is usually the case, plan for migration. At this point, this means factoring into the inventory and audit process an evaluation of content readiness for migration.

Assess phase: As you go through the inventory and audit process, review the content for its quality to determine which content you can:

- **Migrate as is:** Little or no rework is required.
- **Migrate with rework:** Additional rework or edits are required. For example, You may need to update some content, or you may need to resize or reformat images.
- **Don't migrate:** This content is not needed in the new system.

Define phase: Create a content migration strategy. A content migration strategy identifies the approach to use for content migration.

■ Incorporate the audit recommendation (that is, audit content to determine which content can be migrated as is, which can be migrated but requires rework, and which will not be migrated).

■ Define the migration process or approach. For example, decide whether to use an automated or manual process. Automated migration is more difficult when content is unstructured, poorly structured, or embedded in HTML rather than in templates or a CMS. Automated migration works best for structured content.

■ Treat migration as a process and document it the same way you document the content lifecycle. Create a lifecycle for both manually migrated content and automated content. You may have unique lifecycles for each system you migrate from. For example, you may need a lifecycle for assets within a document-asset-management application, or you may require specific considerations for metadata. Metadata should be migrated with the content it supports. Plan for each process, using an approach similar to the one identified in the section titled "Creating the content plan" (p. 98).

■ After you complete the design phase – or, for agile projects, after you complete each iteration – analyze the gap between the existing content and the new design. Use a content matrix for the future-state experience and current-state content inventory for this comparison.

■ Map existing content into new experience and new structure (which may require a series of mapping documents that call out where existing content goes within the new design. You can map existing content by taking the source of the content from the current-state inventory and placing the link/source/system within the appropriate area of the content matrix (which will identify all content in the new design). You can build fields into the content matrix to support this effort.

■ Run any automated migration processes. Automated migration processes includes any process that pulls content from a current or existing experience into a new experience.

■ Conduct any required content clean-up or edit.

■ Reconcile metadata from the existing content into the new system.

■ Run quality assurance tests and content reviews in the new experience. Build a quality assurance effort into your content plan for migrated content. You will need to check each page manually to verify that the content migrated properly, especially for automated content migration efforts.

A few considerations before migrating:

- Failing to understand how much content you have to migrate can translate into missed deadlines and cost overruns.
- Understand the gaps between your current state and the new design to know where you need to create new content.
- All stakeholders must approve the scope of content to be migrated as well as new content to be created.
- Define the process for content migration, and close on this process early in the content planning phase.

Parallel migration and development

While the development team builds a new system – for example, a content management system – certain migration activities can occur. (For example, the define phase steps identified above). You might also pull existing content into a database or other tool, then clean it up and map it to the new design before pulling it into the new system.

To do this, you can use the fields in a content matrix to create the structure for a database (an Access database, for instance). Then map existing content to the database. Once content is pulled into the database, you can edit as necessary and even pull in new content if the copywriting effort is already underway. All these activities can occur while a technology team implements a new system.

After your development team completes implementation, you can pull the finalized content into it from the database. We refer to this process as extraction, transformation, and migration. This approach allows you to to clean up and map content to the new design prior to the system being complete.

Building a migration plan

For planning purposes, outline the content migration to share with the people who must approve, making it clear that the project plan includes only the content listed. If the team later decides to migrate additional content, it will require more time and resources. When your content includes formats other than text, basic images, or PDFs, scope the work involved in migrating. Enlist an expert for multimedia, microsites, or functionality, such as Flash, to assess the level of effort required.

Often, the migration of such content is not migration at all but rather a redesign of the microsite or functionality. Hence, multimedia and formats like Flash are generally not migrated as is. They require rework.

Microsites require a migration strategy as well. And existing campaigns might not retire when a site goes live. Thus, you might have to bring some campaigns that exist in the old design into the new launch.

If you have regional or country-specific sites – perhaps created with significant effort and expense – you may have to retire those sites slowly and justify the integration of the content and the associated costs against the original costs to create and maintain the sites.

Work with the project and traffic manager to ensure a realistic content migration plan. In many cases, you will want to develop a plan where high-priority content gets migrated before a launch and other areas follow later. This approach works especially well with new images or videos that require significant refactoring or recreating.

A content migration plan should also include mapping existing content to new content types. If new content is required, copy decks or a content matrix should capture the new content. Creating new content can begin as soon as the content requirements from the new design are approved. In general, the sooner you start creating new content, the better.

However, do not attempt to migrate content until the new design is approved and you understand how the design and content interact with the technology. You can begin migrating content before the completion of system implementation by capturing content in a template (such as Excel with XML), but not until the content model, design, taxonomy, and architecture are locked down.

Creating a content calendar and new-content planning process

A *content calendar* is a tool with processes to keep it up to date. Sometimes a content calendar is referred to as an editorial calendar, but since many organizations call out specific types of content as editorial, I use the term content calendar. The same goes for the content planning process. In some cases, organizations refer to this as editorial planning. Regardless of the name, a content calendar accounts for the content necessary to keep an experience relevant and up to date.

This calendar provides a snapshot of the content being developed each week, month, and year. Like many other content deliverables and tools, a content calendar exists as a living document that you should update as you identify the need for new content. Link this calendar to the production-plan tool if it is not fully integrated. Plan to meet regularly to review the calendar against what you learn from site metrics, analytics, user feedback, new business needs, industry trends, and emerging technology. All of these will inform future content decisions.

Figure 6.2 shows a snapshot of a content calendar with a weekly schedule.

	Content Calendar – Q4								
	October					November			
	30	7	14	21	28	4	11	18	25
About Us Section	Daily news and updates								
	Ongoing weekly releases for company news that goes with an acquisition (At least one story per week). Content: TBD								
	Daily tweets from the company president (3 per day)								
	Weekly new content for announcements to go in homepage carousel and lead in to stories in the About Us Section								
	Campaign for campus recruitment in careers section. Content: TBD								
	Video: Foundation, Inner city				**Infographic:** Corporate Responsibility			**Video:** Foundation, in Mexico	
		Quarterly Earnings							

Figure 6.2 – Example content calendar

A content calendar should be updated at least quarterly, as it sets the priorities and schedule for all content to be created. I recommend an annual calendar divided into quarters. Depending on the volume of content, you may want to create a weekly or daily calendar.

At the beginning of the year, take a pass at describing the content you think will be necessary for each area of your content experience, which could include internal portal, company website, etc. An enterprise calendar should contain several smaller calendars that roll up into a larger calendar for each line of business or each channel. Try to account for all the content within your enterprise and for each channel that produces unique content. Many organizations also use content calendars for specific focus areas, such as social media.

Updating a calendar is part of ongoing governance. You build the calendar and process in the build phase if none exist. A calendar should be part of the strategic process to keep content relevant and up to date. Design an operational model for performance where analytics – including SEO and social listening – inform content priorities or areas for optimization. Do this at least quarterly. See Figure 6.3 for an example.

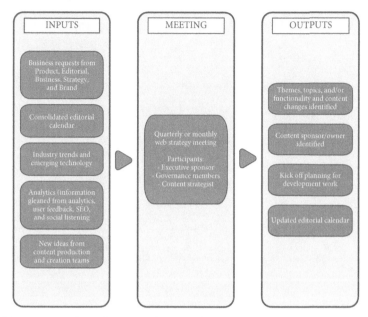

Figure 6.3 – Editorial process for identifying new content and updating a content calendar

Within this process, a quarterly or monthly meeting assesses inputs and informs decisions about future content priorities. By reviewing inputs and content performance, you can create a content planning process where you determine future content areas based on strategic inputs, business goals, and consumer goals. This approach also creates a process less vulnerable to politics and the "highest paid person's opinion," since it ties decisions to analytics and data. Moreover, this process can help future-proof content, keeping it up to date, industry relevant, and responsive to user feedback and needs.

CHAPTER 7
Publish and Measure Phases

Anyone who has written anything or aspires to be writer knows that the word *publish* can bear a profound power. However, within a content strategy, publish functions as a mere step within a content lifecycle where content becomes exposed to an audience. Publish represents the culmination of several steps, and as a step itself, it lives within a larger content lifecycle. In a world where anyone can publish any content online via a blog, tweet, or personal website, the power of the term sometimes becomes lost. But make no mistake, publish does create finality in that the content will be seen, heard, read, and felt by an external audience.

The publish phase brings the content experience to life.

As soon as your content lives in the published or external realm and a consumer can access it, it travels down paths, journeys, and experiences over which you have little control. Tracking the path of your content, its use, and its exposure proves essential to its success.

An effective content strategy requires a performance-driven model, so measuring your content performance ensures a successful, sustainable content experience. By definition, successful content must resonate with a consumer and meet his or her needs. Only through constant evaluation will you know what works and what does not. An effective enterprise content strategy must include a well-defined metrics strategy. Metrics should reflect the strengths and weaknesses of the solution design and provide impetus for content and solution optimization.

This chapter combines the publish and measure phases, since the two go hand-in-hand. It defines measuring content performance, demonstrates how to create metrics, and provides information on reporting.

Definitions
Let's define a few key concepts to frame this effort.

- **Analytics:** The capture and assessment of data, particularly with performance in mind. In the case of enterprise content strategy, analytics includes the measurement of content performance and the analysis of those measurements.

- **Metrics:** Units of measurement. A metric can reflect any kind of measurement. This chapter provides the common metrics used to indicate performance of content, such as the number of consumers who download an article.

- **Key performance indicator (KPI):** A metric used to evaluate the performance of an organization's objectives, for example, the number of products sold.

- **Conversion metrics:** Measurement of a specific conversion, for example, when a content consumer completes a desired task. Typical conversion activities:

  ☐ Purchase a product

  ☐ Add an item to a shopping cart

  ☐ Download a white paper

  ☐ Share a video

  ☐ Create a profile

  ☐ Click to make a call on a smartphone

  ☐ Register a product

A successful metrics strategy begins in the assess, define, and design phases. During those phases, identify the metrics needed to ensure a successful experience so you know exactly what to evaluate after you publish.

Identify metrics early during technology implementation, because you may need to customize your technology solution to track the metrics you need. Some systems require programming or database changes to enable measurement, so identifying metrics early will help avoid delays.

Creating performance metrics

A successful metrics strategy starts with business goals and objectives. A business goal frames a general aspiration to which you create specific, measurable objectives. You should always start with a strategic intent for your experience and a goal.

Let's use a desktop website as an example. In this case, the strategic intent, goals, and objectives of a desktop website might look like this:

- **Strategic intent:** Answer the question "why our company?" in a way that competitively differentiates us for the consumer, investor, career seeker, financial analyst, and media.

- **Goal:** Become the premium website in the industry and go-to source for all products, outperforming all other competitors in purchases, traffic, and brand perception.

- **Objectives:**
  - ☐ Sell X number of products within X amount of time to X audiences.
  - ☐ Generate X number of articles in (names of media) over X time due to exceptional media experience in news and media section.
  - ☐ Increase overall website traffic by X percent by X time.
  - ☐ Increase the amount of socially shared content by X by X time.
  - ☐ Increase number of consumer profiles created by X over X time.

The strategic intent provides an umbrella strategy for the experience; the goal, a lofty aspiration; and the objectives, specific and measurable desired outcomes.

During the plan, assess, and define phases, identify the key criteria for success. At that point, you should identify the strategic intent, goal, and objectives at a high level. Through the design phase, hone them all so each is specific to the solutions you create, down to the page, template or even module level. Metrics will measure whether you meet each of these objectives.

To develop metrics, first look at an objective, and then extract a metric from that objective. Then define what success or finality of the metric means (for example, through analytics applications, dashboards, consumer surveys, conversion rates, or sales reports). Example:

Objective: Increase online sales by X % over X time with X consumers.

Metric: Number of website consumers who purchase a product within a given time period as measured by web analytics and sales data.

Make the metrics as specific as possible by asking these questions:

- **For whom** is the objective targeted? Customers, potential customers, analysts, career seekers, etc. You can also include persona or segment.
- **When or how** will we complete the objective? Example: within 6 months we will sell 20% more products.
- **How many** consumers, products, downloads, piece of content shared, etc., are we aiming for?
- **Where** are we targeting the objective? Example: the geographical location, the channel, or a specific area on the site.
- **Why** are we doing it? Example: to increase sales, to increase downloads, to increase shared content, to increase the number of content consumers.

Incorporate as many of the above points as you can within an objective to make it as specific as possible.

You can also use the SMART approach to develop your objectives. The SMART approach generally applies to setting business goals and objectives, requiring objectives to have these characteristics:

- Specific
- Measurable
- Accountable
- Realistic
- Timely

Example: increase the number of new visitors to the home page by 20% within the next 6 months.

From your objectives, you can glean what to measure. See Table 7.1 for a list of common metrics.

Table 7.1 – Common metrics

Metric	Definition
User/consumer path and clickstream	Measures the path a user takes to complete a task. To use this metric, assume user journeys or paths for the completion of specific tasks (for example, purchase an item or download a white paper). This metric helps you determine what a content consumer does within a journey. This metric helps to validate what you think your consumer journeys are versus the actual path a content consumer takes. For omnichannel experiences, measure this journey across multiple channels.
Length of visit	Captures how long a consumer stays within the experience. For example, how long does a content consumer stay on the website?
Depth of visit	Shows how far a consumer goes into an experience, such as a website. You can also look across channels to see which channels a content consumer engages and where and when.
Conversion	Measures the completion of a task. Many types of conversion metrics exist. You will want to measure number of consumers, tally bounce and exit rates prior to conversion (noting where the exit happens), and review the journey taken to convert. For each conversion metric, create one or more user/consumer journeys.
External keyword search terms	Identifies which terms are used in search, both within your digital experience and through organic search (for example, Google.com, Bing.com). You may want to review both mobile and desktop experiences. Google Analytics or other tools can help track this information. Stay informed regarding changes to algorithms by major search engines, which can render this task difficult.

Metric	Definition
Onsite search keywords	Shows which key terms are used within your digital experience for search, as opposed to an external search engine. These indicate people's interests. Note when a consumer jumps to use online search, often indicating that the consumer cannot find what he or she seeks via navigation. In addition to top search keywords, look at failed searches or searches that return no results. Also note when the consumer refines the search terms, and capture facet usage, if relevant. Preferred search terms (*canine* over *dog*) are another important metric.
Number of visits to convert	Identifies the number of times a consumer leaves and return before converting. Where does the consumer go (if you can track it) upon leaving the experience?
Point of entry	Identifies where a consumer enters the experience or content. This metric may provide a starting point for the consumer journey. How does a content consumer get to the experience: via a keyword search? via a banner ad? via a competitor's site?
Value of interaction	Calculates the total revenue generated from the visit. This metric can be itemized or can account for all visits to the website by dividing the number of visitors by the total revenue.
Cost to convert	Demonstrates how much a conversion costs a business or an organization. This metric looks at internal spending and the total number of conversions as well as revenue of conversions when relevant.
Exit metrics	Measures where a content consumer exits an experience. Note the length of time spent and which device the consumer uses prior to exiting. An exit does not necessarily correlate to a cause for concern; perhaps the visitor accomplished what he or she needed to do and, thus, left your experience satisfied.
Bounce rates	In contrast to exit rates, bounce rates inform you that a visitor reached your experience and left immediately. In other words, a consumer might reach a product-landing page through an external site and – without spending any time there or going further into the experience – "bounce" out of the website by going to a different URL. Track whenever this happens, as well as point of entry, length of time of visit, where the consumer went after, etc. This metric may help you detect under-performing content.
User-interaction history	Indicates how often a consumer visits an experience. What does he or she do while within the experience? For consumers with profiles (users who are logged in), which features, functions, and content do they use?

In addition to the metrics in Table 7.1, you might need to capture social media metrics. Table 7.2 provides some common social metrics:

Table 7.2 – Example social media metrics

Metric	Definition
Post rates	Tracks which content (for example, a product or video on Facebook, Twitter, Tumblr, Pinterest) is shared by whom and when. Look at how often a consumer re-shares the content (for example, by retweeting).
Share of voice	Captures how frequently social media mentions your experience, brand, or organization.
Referrals from social media	Indicates which social media refers visitors to your experience, for example, a link in Twitter that results in a visitor landing on an article on your website.
Social sentiment	Tracks what others are writing about you in social media. Sentiment can be tracked with regard to perception of a brand, an experience such as a website, specific pieces of content such as a video, or even the experience with a product or service.
Repeat engagement	Indicates which consumers, and how many, continue to mention your experience or content, for example, repeat likes within Twitter, repeat shares of your content on Facebook, repeat mentions of your brand or organization, etc.

The metrics in Table 7.2 can all be attained in various ways, including Google Analytics, Bing Analytics, social-tracking tools, and web-analytics software. Additionally, many content management systems include this functionality, and there are applications that track a variety of metrics. In many cases, you may require more than one application.

Operational metrics

So far, I've covered metrics for digital experiences. Obviously, though, digital metrics do not capture all the objectives that an enterprise should measure. Let's consider the following operational metrics, which can prove equally important for showing the value of content within your organization.

- **Reduction in cost to produce content:** Measured by data supplied by business units, internal audits, and operational metrics dashboards
- **Reduction in cost associated with finding and leveraging content within an organization:** Measured by user and consumer surveys, audits, and operational metrics dashboards
- **Reduction in localization cost due to improved processes and systems:** Measured by audits and operational metrics dashboards

- **Cost per word (used in translation cost assessments):** Measured by audits and operational metrics dashboards
- **Time saved authoring, maintaining, and optimizing content:** Measured by user and consumer surveys, audits, and operational metrics dashboards
- **Increase in internal satisfaction with information and content:** Measured by surveys and operational metrics dashboards
- **Decrease in content redundancy:** Measured by user and consumer surveys, audits, and operational metrics dashboards
- **Reduction in cost due to content reuse:** Measured by user and consumer surveys, audits, and operational metrics dashboards
- **Time saved in taking a product to market:** Measured by user and consumer surveys, audits, and operational metrics dashboards
- **Decrease in employee attrition through improved employee tools, self-service tools, and resources (portals):** Measured by user and consumer surveys, audits, and operational metrics dashboards

Content experience metrics

Finally, you should look at other evidence related to content experience. User/consumer/customer feedback, surveys, and user-testing tools can show how your content performs and why content consumers may or may not respond to it.

Additional content experience metrics:

- **Consistent brand experiences with all customer touchpoints (facilitated by content that is on-brand and effectively targeted across multichannel platforms):** Measured by consumer surveys and audits
- **Retention of customers:** Measured by customer databases, sales data, surveys, and audits
- **Acquisition of new customers:** Measured by analytics, sales data, and audits
- **Optimized content quality (means consistent content across channels, free from errors):** Measured by quality standard audits, customer feedback, and time-to-publish updates and modifications
- **Up-to-date, relevant content:** Measured by quality standard audits, customer feedback, and time-to-publish updates and modifications
- **Efficacy of content related to its value proposition and key selling points:** Measured by analytics, testing (for example, A/B testing or multivariate testing), customer feedback, audits, and sales data
- **Improved localized content with fewer errors and revisions:** Measured by quality standard audits

Identifying the types of metrics to capture only provides you with partial success; what you do with the metrics is what really matters. Let's discuss how to analyze metrics data and report on it.

Analyzing and reporting metrics

Metrics provide you with data that helps you draw conclusions about your content and its performance. But metrics by and large do not answer the question *why*? Metrics do not tell you *why* consumers do or do not view or share your content. To find out why, you must dig deeper.

Let's first discuss when and where you should look to answer this question. If content performs well, that is, it's meeting its objectives, then perhaps you will want to produce more content similar to it and make investments in its ongoing success.

When content fails to meet its objectives, you have a problem. Look at every place where content does not perform well. After you have a list of the problem areas – which can be anything from consumer journey to conversion to content not receiving any visitors at all – find the cause. For content not viewed at all, are consumers interested in the topic? Do they seek it out? Are issues in search or navigation preventing them from getting there in the first place? Have you received negative feedback on the content?

When something seems amiss, first check to see if there are issues with the user experience. Then, see how the content performs elsewhere in the industry. Do competitors use the same content? If so, how does it differ from yours? Are there social metrics to indicate interest? You may need user testing to see why content fails to perform successfully. In some cases, you might need to modify your objectives. Maybe, content you consider important is not important to your audience.

As you determine the causes, build and maintain a list of resolutions.

Report to the content team any findings, perhaps using a dashboard. Present internal metrics, track efficiencies, costs, etc. quarterly. For metrics that track your content experience, determine how often you wish to review and present. In many cases, you will want to analyze metrics monthly. In other cases, you might want to do so quarterly. In some larger ecommerce environments, organizations track metrics hourly. Chapter 8, *Optimize Phase*, deals with how to optimize your content based on your findings.

Additional reading

Web Analytics 2.0[11] by Avinash Kaushik is an excellent primer on digital analytics.

I recommend anything written by Eric Peterson and any of the founding members of webanalyticsdemystified.com, which has a wealth of information about web analytics, including free book downloads (e.g., *The Big Book of Key Performance Indicators*).

An excellent resource on search-engine metrics and how to track them: *Search Engine Optimization: All in One for Dummies*[7] by Bruce Clay and Susan Esparza.

For an overview of content performance measurement, including channel engagement for mobile and smartphone, see Rebecca Schneider and Kevin P. Nichols' *Successful Content With a Metrics Driven Approach* (http://www.slideshare.net/kpnichols/content-metrics-drivenap-proach20130410final).

Finally, another great read on the topic is Lou Rosenfeld's *Search Analytics For Your Site*[18].

CHAPTER 8
Optimize Phase

Welcome to the last phase in our content plan lifecycle, *Optimize*! The word sounds impressive for a reason. This phase ensures that your content will remain relevant, contextual, and timely for those who consume it. Here, you determine which content requires your attention, which content to leave as is, and which content you should archive or sunset. This phase reviews all of the learnings from analytics, inputs from the business, industry trends, changes in consumer behavior, and emerging technology to help you improve the content experience.

Because this phase presents a critical juncture in performance-driven content, I want to review the closed-loop lifecycle again. Figure 8.1 demonstrates where the optimize phase fits within the project lifecycle and how it fits into the overall process.

Figure 8.1 – Closed-loop project lifecycle

After you publish content, you should measure its performance. These measurements will help you identify which content performs well and which does not. From that analysis, you can begin to frame a picture of what you need to do. After you identify the opportunities, you start the planning process, and the wheel starts all over again.

This chapter shows you how to optimize content, leave it alone, and/or archive it, and illustrates how an organization supports all three.

Determining which content to optimize, leave as is, or archive

If your content performs satisfactorily – that is, it meets or nearly meets its objectives – you likely will leave the content as it is and update it only if its performance changes. This as-is content obviously yields the easiest solution because it requires no immediate attention. However, most content possesses a shelf life, so at some point this content will require attention. Through quarterly or semiannual assessment, you can determine when this content needs to be refreshed.

For content that performs exceptionally well – let's say an article that many consumers read, download, and share socially above and beyond expectations – you may want to consider investing in similar content, elevating the content by having it appear on a homepage, placing it in additional channels, or developing stories to support it. If the content yields higher conversions or increases the sales of a product, consider developing similar content for other products or services you offer. Look at why the content performs well, and try to uncover the keys to its success so that you can replicate these with your other content.

Things to review:

- **Point of entry:** Where and how do visitors arrive? For example, do visitors consume content as one step in a larger journey? Do they use internal or external keyword searches to get to content? Do they arrive via a link in social media?
- **Topics within the content:** What does the content convey? Which themes, topics, or stories does the content tell? In what format does the content reside (text, PDF, video, etc.)?
- **Social relevance:** Do consumers share your content? How does it trend on social media sites? What do people say about it?
- **Engagement:** Does the content result in conversion? How long does a consumer spend with the content (the duration of interaction)? On which platform/how is the content consumed? What does the consumer do with the content?
- **Competition:** How does your content perform vis-à-vis your competitors? Do they have similar content, or is your content unique?

All of these factors can help you determine why content does or doesn't succeed. Include analytics, usability, social, and search-engine-optimization folks in the conversation, as each will bring a unique viewpoint.

Caution: When content performs well, do not change or move it. You can add it to other areas, but make sure you follow best practices for search engine optimization. Add a summary or a tag-line lead-in to avoid negative reactions from your content consumers.

For content that performs poorly, use the same evaluation to determine why. If you can remove poorly performing content without repercussions, or if you feel that the content adds little value for your consumers, then remove it or place it in an area where the real-estate is less important. For high-priority content critical to your objectives, make every attempt to determine why the content does not perform as it should.

Follow these steps:

1. Does the content receive any visitors at all or is it even found. Perhaps the content quality is good, but its placement in the navigation or on a long, scrolling page makes it impossible to find.
2. If people do view the content, figure out how users engage with it. Do they view the content in its entirety? Do they look at it briefly then leave? Perhaps the content doesn't meet their needs. Maybe the content is published in a manner that makes it difficult to use (long-form articles as opposed to short summaries on a smartphone device, for example, or PDFs instead of HTML pages).
3. If consumers do view the content but you don't get the desired outcome, such as a conversion or the completion of a step within a user journey, then determine whether you need to reassess your user and consumer journeys.
4. Evaluate the content's suitability. Can the consumer easily complete the next step in a journey? Does the consumer find the content useful or relevant? Is the content well-written, on-brand, and free from errors?
5. If all else fails, review your objectives. Perhaps the content is fine but your organization has set unrealistic objectives for it.

Look at competitor sites to see how they use similar content. You may need user testing to finalize your assessment. Make fixes accordingly.

You should archive or delete content that has run its course or proves ineffective. Often, you will set a time-frame for the content after you publish it. For example, you may wish to make certain content only available during a particular season, such as winter.

When you unpublish your content – which in a digital experience means you remove it or take it away from digital consumption (removing a page from a website) – you will likely archive the content. Archiving can require its own strategy, and for many types of business or organizations, an archival process must conform to certain legal requirements.

For example, the Sarbanes–Oxley Act in the United States requires certain businesses, such as financial institutions and public companies, to archive internal and external communications. In this context, archiving means that a system records the content and stores it internally on a server or in a database (or a third-party completes this task and keeps a copy of the content in a secured environment). Several other countries have similar requirements. You should work with a legal team to determine which types of content require continued storage. Your content lifecycle should incorporate these requirements, and you may need technology to support your plans.

For example, if you unpublish content from an internal employee portal, you may need to store it in a searchable, archival database. In some cases, you may be able to delete the content permanently, but I recommend a careful assessment of which content fits this category. You might benefit from retaining a record of the content, even if you see no immediate reason to do so.

A model for successful content planning

Once you assess how your content performs, create an internal process to help you respond to changes in performance, as discussed in the previous chapter. Understanding how this process fits into the optimize phase can help you incorporate it correctly. This model can help you plan and continuously position yourself for success. Figure 8.2 shows how this model works.

Look at the recommendations from the measurement and analysis phases, and inform your plans for future content once a month or quarterly at a minimum. In many cases, monthly or even weekly assessment proves essential. Once you determine your focus areas – that is, the areas you wish to optimize, delete, or archive – you can update the content calendar and initiate projects to execute the ideas.

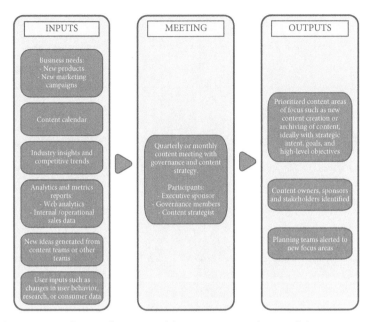

Figure 8.2 – Quarterly or monthly content meeting model

Figure 8.3 demonstrates how you plan for this approach. This diagram displays the entire process for a performance-driven framework.

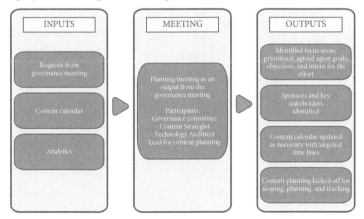

Figure 8.3 – Content planning meeting

Now we have been through the entire enterprise content strategy lifecycle and touched on key considerations within each phase. To keep content and its ecosystem in good shape going forward, you need governance.

CHAPTER 9
Govern Phase

By now, you should understand that content lives within an ecosystem and continually evolves. To thrive, this ecosystem should reside within a caring, well-informed, maintained, and controlled environment. By using governing tools such as standards and a governance committee to seed and feed your content ecosystem, you can guarantee the success of your content. *Governance* supports a consistent, relevant, timely, and effective content experience. Additionally, governance oversees the entire content ecosystem, establishing tools, processes, roles, responsibilities, and ongoing operations.

Governance is not an every-once-in-a-while process, but rather a comprehensive ongoing exercise required for optimal content performance. Think of governance as a rule of law with the constitutional authority and jurisprudence to evolve that law and the organizational means to support the mandates and structure it puts forth. If that sounds a little too authoritarian, then think of content governance as combining the roots that support a unified vision with the influence to get things done.

In enterprise content strategy, governance guides the ongoing strategy for these areas:

- Content strategy
- Content enhancements
- Content lifecycles
- Content planning and editorial strategy
- Digital strategy regarding which content goes into which channel or digital property
- Taxonomy and metadata
- User-generated-content moderation

Governance drives your content strategy. It resides at the center of the lifecycle diagram, represented by the largest circle. Governance ensures that once a content strategy is implemented, it will be maintained and positioned to evolve and grow effectively. Content governance comprises roles (people), processes, and standards. All three are necessary to execute a thorough governance model.

This chapter describes several different governance models, outlines a governance charter, and explains how to implement each within your organization. While not a comprehensive treatment of governance, this chapter will get you started.

Content-governance organizational models

Many organizations have some governance in place to monitor and regulate content. Unfortunately, in my experience, many organizations have not properly implemented governance, especially around content. Often, a website- or digital-governance committee exists, but it may not govern other aspects of content, such as the taxonomy or internal publishing. Therefore, since the web is only one channel, it's usually better for an organization to have one key governance model (perhaps a communication or information governance group) that channel-governance subgroups can be a part of. Governance plays a critical role in content decisions, so it must be established immediately as part of the kick-off of a content strategy.

All content deliverables described in this book should receive approval from the governance committee. The sooner you create a governance committee, the better. The content team can function as an ad hoc governance committee, but you will most likely need a more formal structure to provide ongoing oversight.

When creating a governance structure, you should first determine which type of structure will best support the organization's needs. Traditionally, two models were used in content governance: centralized and federated. But today, given the demands of global and decentralized organizations, which must maintain brand standards while providing autonomy to business units across the globe, a hybrid model has emerged as an alternative. While other models exist, these three are the most widely used:

- **Centralized:** All content, strategies, and processes are controlled by a centralized authority.
- **Federated:** Different business units or regions within a global enterprise govern their own content, strategies, and processes.
- **Hybrid:** All content, strategies, and processes are controlled by a single source, but each line of business or region writes and recommends standards for its own content. These roll up to the centralized authority. A certain amount of autonomy is allowed but only within an agreed-upon structure that defines what is centralized and what is federated.

Regardless of the type of model your organization chooses, a content governance model should contain the following roles:

- **Executive sponsor:** The evangelist for content governance throughout the enterprise. The executive sponsor is the ultimate escalation point for arbitration on unresolved issues by the governance committee.
- **Governance committee:** A group comprising multiple stakeholders and content owners. The governance committee oversees all aspects of content governance.
- **Working groups:** These groups support the committee by creating the standards, documentation, and processes that the governance committee approves.

A typical governance model is presented in Figure 9.1.

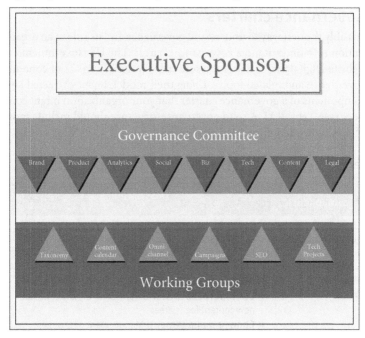

Figure 9.1 – Typical governance model

In this example, an executive sponsor sits at the top of the structure. Below are distinct lines of business (brand, product, analytics, etc.) that make up the governance committee. Working groups sit under the governance committee and report into it.

Because each organization is different, it is hard to say from the outside which model best suits an organization. Some require a tight, centralized model to manage and execute consistent standards. Other organizations are hindered by centralization and need a federated approach where decisions can be made without a centralized authority.

Increasingly, many organizations need standardization, while at the same time, they must provide autonomy for business units or regions outside the central authority. This need rings especially true for global businesses that have a presence in many countries.

Even if an organization is not international, it may face similar challenges. For example, a university with many different schools will run into the same issues. Regardless, a strong executive sponsor is essential to help build buy-in for the model.

Governance charters

Possibly the best way to understand governance and its role in an organization is to understand a governance charter. The US Government website Digitalgov[1] is a useful resource for information about content governance and related topics. Using their model, I have extracted key components of a governance charter that your organization might consider (see Table 9.1). A solid governance structure should include most of these considerations.

Table 9.1 – Components of a governance charter

Charter component	Description
Objective of the governance charter	■ Sets the scope, roles, composition, and responsibilities ■ Identifies the goals of governance ■ Defines the key objectives of governance
Purpose of the governance board	■ **Compliance:** Adherence to standards and processes ■ **Content focus areas:** Identification of new content or new content focus areas ■ **Change management:** Management of changes ■ **Risk management:** Management of risks ■ **Performance:** Measurement of governance performance and solution performance ■ **Setting strategy and policies:** What is the strategy for content? ■ **Accountability:** Who is accountable for what? What is the escalation process and path?

---

[1] http://www.digitalgov.gov/category/managing-digital/governance/

Charter component	Description
Roles and responsibilities	■ Who is on the board, and what do they govern? ■ What are the main stakeholders and working groups? ■ What do stakeholders oversee? ■ What is the escalation path? (An organizational chart may prove useful.)
Expectations of membership	■ Expectation for attendance ■ Procedures for making decision (rules for absences and voting by proxy)
Governance scope	■ What is governed by committee? ■ Which tools and standards support governance?
Executive sponsorship	■ Who owns the governance (the website) from an executive standpoint? ■ Who is the final decision maker in the escalation path?
Board values and principles	■ **Values:** What are the guiding principles and vision? ■ **Norms:** When, how often, and where are meetings?
Reporting	■ Who receives governance meeting minutes? ■ Who records the minutes?

Creating governance in your organization

If your organization does not possess a content-governance plan, you face issues like these:

■ A proliferation of microsites to meet short-term needs that then live on in perpetuity.

■ Inconsistent, off-brand external-facing content.

■ Lines of business doing what they want with content in the absence of standards.

■ Difficulties getting traction on new projects.

■ And the list goes on and on....

Be the champion of good content governance. Here are the steps to creating governance:

1. Decide on a governance model.
2. Agree on what is necessary for a charter.
3. Define when the participants will meet, agendas for those meetings, and how strategy will be implemented.

By using steps similar to those described in Chapter 2, *Plan Phase*, for creating a content team, you can create a governance team. Always remember, governance ensures the success of your content and is the backbone of any robust content ecosystem.

Additional resources

The topic of governance warrants its own book, and Lisa Welchman is writing it. *Managing Chaos: Digital Governance by Design* is slated for publication in late 2014. Given the quality of her thought leadership, I am confident in recommending this book prior to reading it. In addition, Lisa has written and spoken extensively on the topic. Her blog and papers can be found here: http://welchmanpierpoint.com/.

The Karr.net website's Governance Encyclopedia[2] contains a goldmine of information on governance.

Ann Rockley and Charles Cooper also cover the topic of governance in *Managing Enterprise Content: A Unified Content Strategy*[17].

---

[2] http://www.karr.net/website_governance/encyclopedia.htm

CHAPTER 10
Conclusion

Enterprise content strategy continues to evolve. As themes like omni-channel and performance-driven content – not to mention future technological advances – become mainstream, the practices advocated in this book will become more important.

This guide provides a blueprint for best practices in enterprise content strategy. While it is not an exhaustive guide, it offers what I believe is a solid and robust approach for anyone who wants to learn more about creating effective content solutions. By applying the principles described in this book – and by using works such as Ann Rockley and Charles Cooper's book[17] – you will be able to create effective, resilient, lasting content experiences supported by a strong and nimble content ecosystem.

Thank you for taking the time to read my book. I wish you success in establishing better and stronger content processes and experiences!

And a final note: If you wish to engage in further dialogue or you have questions regarding any of the ideas presented in this book, feel free to reach out to me at kevinpnichols.com or @kpnichols on Twitter. I am happy to help in any way I can to assist you as you go down the journey of practicing content strategy. At the very least, I will help point you in the right direction. I promise you that I will continue to advance the ideas expressed in this book, so check my website often for more thought leadership in content strategy! Thanks again and I wish you the best.

Kevin P. Nichols,
October 2014

Acknowledgments

This guide could not have been written without the exhaustive help of Rebecca A. Schneider (azzardconsulting.com) and Alexa D. O'Brien (alexaobrien.com). Both Rebecca and Alexa provided insights based on their subject matter expertise and helped edit this document. Alexa contributed countless hours to this entire document, and she edited, formatted, and goosed me into getting the original manuscript completed. Laura Lerner and Julie Christie, then took the manuscript and made significant recommendations overall. After that period, I did little work on it up until Sapient said they would help me publish it as an ebook. Then Lauren Cohen helped me get it into even better shape.

Last year, I received a call from Scott Abel asking me if I had any book ideas for a series he was creating. After I signed a contract with XML Press, thanks to Richard Hamilton, Scott and Richard assigned Laura Creekmore as the executive editor. Laura inspired me to turn this work into a project guide, and she worked on several versions of edits to help me get it there. Richard Hamilton also provided a lot of assistance and feedback, and I am very grateful he put up with me.

I had the book peer reviewed again with Paula Land, Noreen Compton, Timothy Truxell, Steven Grindlay, Laura Blaydon, Rahel Bailie, and Anne Casson. Others to thank include: Lisa Kile, Lisa Copeland, Max Shapiro, Ben Royce, Mark Chelius, Donald Chesnut, David Cohen, Karen L Machart – an amazing visual designer – and Trey DeGrassi. Special thanks to Cynthia O'Brien at Market Street Bookstore in Mashpee, Ma. I'd also like to offer a special thank you to Patricia Melson at the United Airlines Club in Boston for making my life just a little bit easier.

A very huge thank you to my entire content strategy team at Sapient-Nitro. Working with all of you has been a highlight in my professional career, and your interactions with me have shaped this book.

I would also like to thank Dr. Mark J Hirsch for his continual support and my parents, Mary and Paul Nichols. Ann Rockley provides the foreword and she too provided her input, which is greatly appreciated. Finally, I'm grateful to Marcia Riefer Johnston, author of *Word Up!*[10], for the copy edits – and for going beyond copy editing to help shape this book. I will insist that she be involved with any book I write in the future.

Glossary

analytics

Website traffic and usage statistics, typically capturing data such as how many users have viewed a page, how long users stay on pages, the pages through which users enter or exit a site, and the paths through which users traverse the site.

content

Any text, image, video, decoration, or user-consumable elements that contribute to comprehension.

content brief

A summary of your plan for a content project. For large projects, a content brief summarizes your plan for each project phase.

content calendar

A tool used to plan content within an organization. A content calendar shows the content publishing schedule for an organization during a calendar period (E.g., annual, monthly, weekly, etc).

content experience

The emotional experience created by content for a consumer.

content management system

A software application that supports information capture, editorial, governance, and publishing processes with tools such as workflow, access control, versioning, search, and collaboration.

content model

A formal representation of structured content as a collection of content types and their interrelationships.

content type

A specification for a structured, standardized, reusable, and mutually exclusive kind of information entity.

controlled vocabulary

A standardized approach for labeling and organizing content. A controlled vocabulary contains a set of standardized labels (and often preferred alternative terms), and it illustrates the relationships between each term. A controlled vocabulary underpins a successful enterprise content strategy design. Controlled vocabularies form the foundation of metadata schemas. As the name implies, a controlled vocabulary controls and sets the standards for the vocabulary an organization uses. A taxonomy is a type of controlled vocabulary.

faceted taxonomy
Aspects of content that can be used in a taxonomy to describe overarching themes, such as content type, audience, subject, geographic region, language, and action. Each facet creates multiple pathways to access information. Faceted taxonomies lend themselves well to a digital format and allow a content consumer to navigate via many pathways and still retrieve the desired result. For example, paint can be represented by color, finish (flat, semigloss), use (indoor, outdoor, basement), and additives (grit, anti-mold). On a website that sells paint, a consumer can find paint using one or more of these facets.

governance
The systems, policies, and processes used to manage and control a content set to ensure consistency, efficiency, and compliance with standards.

intelligent content
Structurally-rich and semantically-categorized content that is, therefore, automatically discoverable, reusable, reconfigurable, and adaptable.

metadata
"The data about the data." Metadata enables system integration, allows for more accurate and targeted search engine results, drives parametric/guided navigation, enables dynamic content, and facilitates personalization on internal and external websites. Metadata fosters content intelligence (meaning the mechanism that allows for building logic into content). An enterprise content strategy uses metadata to find the highest quality and most relevant content to display to the right user at the right time and in the most efficient manner possible.

On an enterprise content strategy project, metadata stands as the force behind delivering high-quality, relevant content experiences. A strong metadata schema allows systems to communicate with each other, drives search engines, and enables intelligent-content solutions, such as personalization. Well-designed metadata can often dramatically improve content lifecycles and even makes day-to-day life easier for people working with content. Content strategy expert Rachel Lovinger reinforces the importance of metadata to content strategy in her presentation "Make Your Content Nimble." Metadata values can derive from a taxonomy, a thesaurus, or other controlled vocabulary.

multichannel

A multichannel content strategy addresses the various publication or distribution points at which content will be accessed by users and ensures that the experience is relevant in each context.

omnichannel

An evolution of multichannel that focuses on the consumer's point of view at each step in his or her interaction with your content. It looks at online and offline content, regardless of channel. Instead of simply delivering the same content through multiple channels, a true omnichannel experience creates a consumer journey that accounts for where, when, and why a consumer jumps from one channel to another to complete a task.

ontology

A representation of relationships between terms or concepts. These defined relationships can express a greater range of associations than a simple hierarchy (taxonomy). Ontologies are most often used for semantic navigation, semantic grouping, and the semantic web. For more information, see wikipedia.org/wiki/semantic_web. An excellent starting point for ontologies is Natalya F. Noy's and Deborah L. McGuinness' "Ontology Development 101: A Guide to Creating Your First Ontology."

parametric search

A search that uses a set of parameters to help narrow or filter results. Faceted taxonomies are required to support parametric search and navigation. An example of parametric search is kayak.com, which enables people to filter a search-engine query by airline, flight time, price, etc.

personalization

The practice of targeting content to users based on one or more of the following: who they are; where they are; when, why, and how they access the content; and what device they use to access it.

synonym ring

Equivalent terms. A group of words that convey the same meaning. A synonym ring employs different terms that a content consumer would use to identify the same piece of information. A synonym ring can be created in a metadata schema. Example: *cat, kitty, feline,* etc. A synonym ring identifies multiple terms for a desired result. Not all content consumers would identify a given piece of information with the same label. Synonym rings and thesauri are often used behind the scenes to improve enterprise or website searches.

taxonomy
The art of stuffing animals and putting them on a mantelpiece. (Just seeing if you are paying attention.) Taxonomy is the science of organizing, categorizing, or classifying information. Typical types include hierarchical taxonomy, faceted taxonomy, and folksonomy. A department store provides a good example of organizing information by a taxonomy: clothing is often organized by gender, then designer, then clothing type, and so forth. A music store offers another example, often classifying music into categories by genre, then alphabetically by artist (dance, Madonna). The organization of food in a grocery store provides another example: Flank steak is grouped by meat, then under beef, then by its cut. Any type of product catalog classification representing a company's wares is generally organized using a taxonomy.

thesaurus
A tool that presents a list of terms and shows the relationships between synonyms and other related terms (for example, *broad* and *narrow*). A thesaurus organizes information with a preferred term, broader and narrower terms, and equivalent terms. For additional reading on thesauri construction, visit the University of Western Ontario's *Tutorial on Thesaurus Construction.* [4]

---

[4] http://publish.uwo.ca/%7Ecraven/677/thesaur/main00.htm

Bibliography

[1] Abel, Scott and Rahel Bailie, editors. *The Language of Content Strategy*. XML Press. 2014. http://thecontentstrategybook.com.

[2] Aitchison, Jean, Alan Gilchrist, and David Bawden. *Thesaurus Construction and Use: A Practical Manual*. Europa Publications. 4th ed. 2000.

[3] Bailie, Rahel and Noz Urbina. *Content Strategy: Connecting the dots between business, brand, and benefits*. XML Press. 2013.

[4] Bloomstein, Margot. *Content Strategy at Work: Real-world Stories to Strengthen Every Interactive Project*. Morgan Kaufmann. 2012. http://appropriateinc.com/book/.

[5] Casson, Anne and Kevin Nichols. *SapientNitro Content Strategy 2013 Positioning*. SapientNitro. June, 2013. http://www.kevinpnichols.com/enterprise_content_strategy/.

[6] Colman, Jonathon. "Epic List of Content Strategy Resources." www.jonathoncolman.org/2013/02/04/content-strategy-resources/.

[7] Clay, Bruce and Susan Esparza. *Search Engine Optimization All-in-One For Dummies*. 2nd ed. For Dummies. 2012. Third edition is scheduled for November, 2014.

[8] Halvorson, Kristina and Melissa Rach. *Content Strategy for the Web*. 2nd ed. New Riders. 2012.

[9] Hedden, Heather. *The Accidental Taxonomist*. Information Today. 2010.

[10] Johnston, Marcia Riefer. *Word Up! How to Write Powerful Sentences and Paragraphs (And Everything You Build from Them)*. Northwest Brainstorms Publishing. 2013.

[11] Kaushik, Avinash. *Web Analytics 2.0*. Sybex. 2009. webanalytics20.com.

[12] Land, Paula Ladenburg. *Content Audits and Inventories: A Handbook*. XML Press. 2014.

[13] Lovinger, Rachel. "Make Your Content Nimble." www.slideshare.net/rlovinger/make-your-content-nimble.

[14] Lovinger, Rachel. "Nimble: a razorfish report on publishing in the digital age." nimble.razorfish.com/publication/?m=11968amp;l=1.

[15] Nichols, Kevin and Donald Chesnut. *UX for Dummies*. For Dummies. 2014.

[16] Noy, Natalya Fridman and Deborah L. McGuinness. "Ontology Development 101: A Guide to Creating Your First Ontology." Stanford Knowledge Systems Laboratory Technical Report KSL-01-05 and Stanford Medical Informatics Technical Report SMI-2001-0880. March 2001. www-ksl.stanford.edu/people/dlm/papers/ontology-tutorial-noy-mcguinness.pdf

[17] Rockley, Ann and Charles Cooper. *Managing Enterprise Content: A Unified Content Strategy.* 2nd ed. New Riders Press. 2012.

[18] Rosenfeld, Louis. *Search Analytics for Your Site.* Rosenfeld Media. 2011. rosenfeldmedia.com/books/search-analytics/.

[19] Stewart, Darin L. *Building Enterprise Taxonomies.* Mokita Press. 2008.

About the Author

Kevin Nichols (@kpnichols) is an award-winning thought leader, digital-industry enthusiast, and author with more than 19 years of professional experience. As leader of one of the oldest global content strategy teams, Kevin has grown that team to become one of the largest and most successful in the world. Kevin has been a forerunner and major contributor to user experience and content strategy. He has authored numerous articles on content strategy, user experience, and digital strategy. You can learn more about him at kevinpnichols.com.

In 2014, he coauthored (with Donald Chesnut) *UX For Dummies*[15].

Index

A

Abel, Scott, 16
acquire lifecycle step, 71
adaptive vs. responsive design, 86
agile projects
  process for, 14–15
  stories, 97
Aitchison, Jean, 96
analysis
  competitive and industry, completing, 46–48
  metrics, 114
analytics
  described, 107, 133
  questions to ask stakeholders, 35–36
  role in evaluating success, 118
analytics area, responsibilities during plan phase, 18
annual reports, as content type, 65
architect (technology), in plan phase, 19
archive lifecycle step, 71
archiving content, 118–120
assess (discovery) phase
  completing assessment work, 48
  completing competitive and industry analyses during, 46–48
  conducting content inventories and audits during, 40–46
  content migration during, 100
  gaining understanding of, 27–28
  objective of, 7
  questions to ask stakeholders, 28–39
  reading list, 48
assessments, current-state, 15
assumptions for projects, identifying, 24
audits (content)
  conducting, 40–46
  documenting, 53–55
automation, content migration, 101

B

Bailie, Rahel, 16
batches, sign-off, 97–98
Bawden, David, 96
best practices, defining for projects, 23
biographies, as content type, 65
blog posts, as content type, 66
Bloomstein, Margot, 16, 96
bounce rates, 111
brands, impact of content on, 4
brief, content, 75
budgets for projects, documenting, 24
build phase, 97–105
business analyst (BA), participation in plan phase, 19
business strategy, questions to ask stakeholders, 29
business-unit content ownership area, responsibilities during plan phase, 18

C

calendar (content), creating, 103–105
calendar listings, as content type, 65
Casson, Anne
  definition of content strategy by, 4–5
  on properly executed assess (discovery) phases, 27
  top-10 list of when clients need content strategists, 10
CAT (Content Analysis Tool), 41
centralized governance model, 124
charters
  governance, 126–127
  project, 22–25
Clay, Bruce, 115
clickstream, 110
closed-loop lifecycle, 9, 117
Colman, Jonathon, 16
committees, governance, 124–126
communication, content present in, 4

as factor in enterprise content strategy, 5

building logic into, 83–85

creating strategic intent for, 61–62

described, 2–3

omnichannel and multichannel, designing for, 85–89

questions to ask stakeholders, 37–38

experience with content, defining with user journeys, 88

external keyword search terms, 110

extraction, transformation, and migration approach, 102

F

faceted taxonomies, 92

FAQs (frequently asked questions), as content type, 65

federated governance model, 124

fields to capture during content inventories and audits, 42–46

findings from content audits, writing about, 53–55

Flash, migration of, 102

format-free content, 88

forms, as content type, 65

frameworks

for content strategy, creating, 49–56

for successful content, 87–88

frequently asked questions (FAQs), as content type, 65

future-proofing content solutions, 11

G

Gilchrist, Alan, 96

glossary, as content type, 65

goals of projects, defining, 22

govern phase, objective of, 9

governance

as factor in enterprise content strategy, 5

charters for, 126–127

creating in organizations, 127

described, 123–124, 134

models of, 124–126

questions to ask stakeholders, 39

reading list, 128

role of content calendars in, 104

governance committees, 124–126

Governance Encyclopedia, 128

Grindlay, Steven, on communication's presence with content, 4

guides, as content type, 66

H

Halvorson, Kristina, 15

Hedden, Heather, 96

help content, as content type, 66

high-level roadmaps, designing, 56–59

high-level scope, defining for projects, 23

hiring enterprise content strategists, 9–10

history, user interaction, 111

hybrid governance model, 124

I

images, as content type, 65

implement phase, objective of, 8

index, as content type, 65

industry analysis, completing, 46–48

infographics, as content type, 65

instructions, as content type, 65

intelligent content, building into content experience, 83–85

intent (strategic)

creating at page level, 73–75

creating for content experience, 61–62

interaction history, user, 111

interaction, value of, 111

international/ management area, responsibilities during plan phase, 18

internationalization

questions to ask stakeholders, 32–33

internationalization area, responsibilities during plan phase, 19

interviews with stakeholders, 28–39

inventories (content)

conducting, 40–46

questions to ask stakeholders, 30

inventory applications, validating results from, 45

J

journeys (user), defining content experiences with, 88

K

key performance indicator (KPI), 108

Colophon

About the Book

This book was authored, edited, and indexed in a Confluence wiki. Contents were exported to DocBook using the Scroll DocBook Exporter from K15t Software. The book was then generated from that output using the DocBook XML stylesheets with XML Press customizations and, for the print edition, the RenderX XEP formatter.

About the Content Wrangler Content Strategy Book Series

The Content Wrangler Content Strategy Book Series from XML Press provides content professionals with a road map for success. Each volume provides practical advice, best practices, and lessons learned from the most knowledgeable content strategists in the world. Visit the companion website for more information contentstrategybooks.com.

About XML Press

XML Press (xmlpress.net) was founded in 2008 to publish content that helps technical communicators be more effective. Our publications support managers, social media practitioners, technical communicators, and content strategists and the engineers who support their efforts.

Our publications are available through most retailers, and discounted pricing is available for volume purchases for educational or promotional use. For more information, send email to orders@xmlpress.net or call us at (970) 231-3624.

The Content Wrangler
Content Strategy Book Series

The Content Wrangler Content Strategy Book Series from XML Press provides content professionals with a road map for success. Each volume provides practical advice, best practices, and lessons learned from the most knowledgeable content strategists in the world.

The Language of Content Strategy

Scott Abel and Rahel Anne Bailie

Available Now

Print: $19.95
eBook: $16.95

The Language of Content Strategy is the gateway to a language that describes the world of content strategy. With fifty-two contributors, all known for their depth of knowledge, this set of terms forms the core of an emerging profession and, as a result, helps shape the profession. The terminology spans a range of competencies with the broad area of content strategy.

Content Audits and Inventories: A Handbook

Paula Ladenburg Land

Available Now

Print: $24.95
eBook: $19.95

Successful content strategy projects start with knowing the quantity, type, and quality of existing assets. Paula Land's new book, *Content Audits and Inventories: A Handbook*, shows you how to begin with an automated inventory, scope and plan an audit, evaluate content against business and user goals, and move forward with a set of useful, actionable insights.

Global Content Strategy: A Primer

Val Swisher

Available Now

Print: $19.95
eBook: $16.95

Nearly every organization must serve customers around the world. *Global Content Strategy* describes how to build a global content strategy that addresses analysis, planning, development, delivery, and consumption of global content that will serve customers wherever they are.

Author Experience: Bridging the gap between people and technology in content management

Rich Yagodich

Available Now

Print: $24.95
eBook: $19.95

Author Experience focuses on the challenges of managing the communication process effectively. It deals with this process from the point of view of those who create and manage content. This book will help you define and implement an author experience that improves quality and efficiency.

ContentStrategyBooks.com
XMLPress.net

CPSIA information can be obtained at www.ICGtesting.com
Printed in the USA
BVOW11s1346080115

382387BV00004B/6/P